T0278801

FURY

THE GERMAN LIST

FURY

ELFRIEDE JELINEK

TRANSLATED BY GITTA HONEGGER

INTRODUCED BY MILIND BRAHME

Seagull
BOOKS

LONDON NEW YORK CALCUTTA

Seagull Books, 2022

Originally published as *Wut*
© Elfriede Jelinek, 2016

Performing rights: Rowohlt Theater Verlag, Reinbek
Published by permission of Rowohlt Verlag GmbH, Reinbek

First published in English translation by Seagull Books, 2022
English translation © Gitta Honegger, 2022

ISBN 978 1 8030 9 032 0

British Library Cataloguing-in-Publication Data
A catalogue record for this book is available from the British Library.

Typeset by Seagull Books, Calcutta, India
Printed and bound in the USA by Integrated Books International

CONTENTS

INTRODUCTION

MILIND BRAHME

In December 2020, a court in France convicted and sentenced 14 people for their involvement in the January 2015 attacks on the staff of the French satirical magazine *Charlie Hebdo*, and on Hyper Cacher, a kosher supermarket in Paris. Nine co-workers of the magazine (or was it 8 plus 1 bodyguard?)—reporters and illustrators, a maintenance worker, a policeman, a policewoman, four customers of the supermarket—all Jews—and the two plus one attackers who claimed to owe allegiance to the Al Qaeda in the Arabian Peninsula (AQAP) had all lost their lives in a killing spree spread over three days. The girlfriend (or perhaps wife?) of one of the attackers had fled France a few days before the attacks to Syria (or to Iraq?) and is still wanted by French law-enforcement authorities.

It is by now widely known that the attack on *Charlie Hebdo* was an attack by religious fundamentalists seeking revenge. "We defend the Prophet. If someone offends the Prophet, then there is no problem—we can kill him." This is what one of the attackers said in an interview to a French TV channel during the stand-off with the French security forces. The stand-off ended with both he and the second attacker—his brother—being killed as they emerged from their hide-out, hell bent upon not surrendering, preferring instead to being "martyred" in the cause of "their" religion.

Seen the world over as an attack on the freedom of expression, on freedom of the press, and particularly in

France as an attack on the almost sacred idea of Laïcité—the strict separation of the Church/religion and the State/a public sphere—the killings were almost universally condemned as acts of terror. Although government after government condemned the "terror" and the "violence" and expressed solidarity with France, no one other than the prime minister of Israel seems to have called it an act of "Islamic terror."[1]

Looking at the entire episode from an India caught in a rapid degeneration of the secularity of its own public sphere—though distinctly different from the French version of it—one tended to despair at multiple levels. It seemed deeply hopeless that "in the 21st century, we were still seeing violent confrontation over whose God was 'the best!' "[2] One could not pretend to be blind either to the inflexibility of the French version of secularism—France's faith in and veneration of Laïcité appeared so dogmatic that any questioning of it seemed to border on sacrilege or blasphemy! The suppression and violent domination of the largely Islamic Middle East by Israel and the United States, and the political appeal of religious extremism that was hand in glove with Western conservative politics in each seeking to destroy the "other"[3] further added to the sense of hopelessness and anguish.

---

1 See the Wikipedia entry on 'International Reactions to the *Charlie Hebdo* Shooting'.

2 'Paris Magazine Attack: Search for Gunmen Enters Second Night—As It Happened', *Guardian*, 8 January 2015. Available at: https://bityl.co/CFEO (last accessed on 17 May 2022).

3 'Paris Magazine Attack'.

In *Fury*, psycho-pathological states of consciousness underlying such acts of violence metamorphose through the imagination of the writer-narrator into a breathless, overwhelming flood of words and sentences—a desperate groping in the darkness of the abyss to find or create images, word pictures. Jelinek traverses historical time from ancient Greek mythology to contemporary TV and internet advertisements to *see* and to *show* the blindness of the fury. A blindness precipitated by the hyper-narcissism of a Self that forecloses any possibilities of a hermeneutic understanding of the Other, of the basic togetherness of the I and Thou.

Jelinek's first play, *Was geschah, nachdem Nora ihren Mann verlassen hatte* (What Happened After Nora Left her Husband), written in 1979 "as a reflection upon the centennial of Henrik Ibsen's *A Doll's House* [. . . a] *deconstruction* of its idealistic implications, the heroic strength of the heroine and the utopian hopes for the equality in the partnership of the married couple"[4] (emphasis added) already reflects a language scepticism that is at the heart of so much Austrian writing, filling it with ambi-valence and giving it a self-reflexive character. In *Nora*, the post-revolution disillusionment reveals the degeneration of revolutionary ideas into shallow and hollow slogans. Seen as if in a kaleidoscope alongside the Brechtian V-Effekt (the alienation effect), Ödön von Horváth's *Demaskierung des Bewusstseins* (unmasking of consciousness) and the post-dramatic theatre of Heiner Mueller, Jelinek's "theatre" text allows the reader to experience a literariness which is quite independent of its performative aspect.

---

4 Christine Kiebuzinska, 'Elfriede Jelinek's Nora Project: Or What Happens When Nora Meets the Capitalists', *Modern Drama* 41(1) (Spring 1998): 134–45.

In an insightful interview with her authorized English translator, Gitta Honegger, Jelinek talks about her desire that her "theatre" texts "get read":

> But I also want my plays to exist as [complete] texts and that they get read, but that hasn't happened. Because for the reading audience those are still plays, and plays are hardly read by the general reading audience. But my plays are texts, basically like the novels, just that the ones are texts for speaking, the others for reading. And that's the only difference. The methods are the same.[5]

Clearly Jelinek's plays / theatre texts / performance texts intend to offer the recipient both possibilities—of experiencing them on stage, or reading them as "complete" texts, delving into the stream of consciousness of the writer-narrator as she "speaks to others, *probably always speak[ing] to herself, into herself*" (*Three Plays* 528, emphasis added).

Listening to this writer-narrator speaking to and into herself, or reading her texts is an experience that disturbs, irritates, at times stuns the audience out of a deadened auto-response mode of dealing with our world, which has become a "farcicatastrophical global political reality show."[6] The texts are very often immediate responses to horrific events that no

---

5 Elfriede Jelinek, *Three Plays: Rechnitz, The Merchant's Contracts, Charges (The Supplicants)* (Gitta Honegger trans.) (London: Seagull Books, 2019), p. 549. Henceforth references in parentheses in the text.

6 Gitta Honegger, Introduction to Elfriede Jelinek, *On the Royal Road* (Gitta Honegger trans.) (London: Seagull Books, 2019), p. *ix*.

longer horrify us, the infuriatingly numb "us" who inhabit, watch and play out the global "farcicatastrophy."

Coming back to *Fury*: The inability, or rather the unwillingness to accept the togetherness of the self and the other, the fanatical belief in a binary between us and them—the conviction that the elimination of the other is one's only means of survival—runs through the text. So does the unmasking of a competitive religiosity. Such constant reiteration of this "spirit of competition" drives home the complete disconnect between institutionalized religion and the basic human religious impulse of love and solidarity. So blinding is the grandeur of one's *own* God that one becomes blind to everybody and everything else around.

In fact, blindness, the inability, or rather the unwillingness, of the perpetrators of the violence to SEE—what they are doing and for what reason, as well as to whom and with what consequence—is mirrored by the writer-narrator's inability to put herself into the mindset of those murderers, to understand what's going on inside them (*Fury* 114) and hence to make any sense of what she is witnessing.

> because everybody is always in such a rage, it close[s] their mind [. . .] Anyone who's got a problem finds a repairman and that is usually God, yes, but which one? [. . .] we ha[ve] no way to know. All the better. *It tears doubt apart: That's fury!* [. . .] it puts you in a daze and you don't know what you are doing, but you keep doing it nonetheless. *I don't know now where I am. I don't know who my friends are and where they are, far away or close, better far away, otherwise I might kill them too* and then I'd have no

more friends, that would be a shame, wouldn't it? (*Fury* 94, emphasis added)

[. . .] fury knows no doubt, there is no time for it, second thoughts come first, if at all, it's too late afterwards; [. . .] Like those men I am also incredibly mad at, *but in my blindness I can't see* (*Fury* 95, emphasis added).

While blindness is key to fury, it is also a carefully crafted blindness; customized individually, it cannot be bought off the shelf like any industrially mass-produced product.

So where does it come from?

Cut off we sit in our own house, at a loss. (*Fury* 41) [. . .] are they the guys we wanted to kill? *I can see the trigger and I know how to use it and what's going to happen*, but still, we ask ourselves, where did such fury get a hold of us? Where did such raging come from and become all the rage? Where was it? *Where did it ruin us? Whose ruin did we bring about?* (*Fury* 96)

Through the text, the reader keeps bumping into this "we" and wonders: Who is this we? And which is this house that was always open? Are the WE the "good people" of the West/Europe whose houses are open to the Others, and that's why "they" are here? Was this house truly always open? If yes, for whom?

At one level, *Fury* also appears to be an attempt to sort out through words/text the panic and the bafflement of the inheritors of the Enlightened West as they try and make sense of the violence that is now at their doorstep. Jelinek describes vividly the violence unleashed by the perpetrators.

Her gallows humor blends effortlessly with fascinating descriptions of the weapons used for the acts of violence. And a list of weapons used elsewhere by those in Toyota pick-ups—"flame throwers and a rocket launcher and an anti-tank missile and a cage, where the burning can take place, or an atomic bomb, everything can be done much more efficiently with an atomic bomb" (*Fury* 43). However, reading from an 'other' perspective, one misses other weapons—maybe not an atomic bomb, but tanks and drones and so-called precision bombs, weapons of a different kind of colonization in our postcolonial times.

From the crucifixion to the crusades, from the Thirty Years War to the genocidal violence of colonization, the violence of the Ottoman Empire, the two world wars, the Holocaust and the atom bomb—an unending chain of murderers, "those worthless animals as opposed to a human being . . ." (*Fury* 117). Who exactly then is the writer-narrator indicting here as a non-human worthless animal? Does the writer-narrator agree with Ghassan Hage when he calls this violence "Islamo-fascism"? Of course, such violence, or for that matter all violence, must be unequivocally condemned. However, it is equally true that one must never forget that so-called terror attacks do not happen in an historical vacuum. For many a reader in the postmodern non- West, the horror of the present violence and the traumatic memory of violence perpetrated through history are simultaneous events. Is then such readers' hesitation to immediately condemn each act of "terrorist" violence without a simultaneous reference to the history of violence a sign of ethical bankruptcy? Is the "butchery in Paris and in Vienna" rooted, xiv | MILIND BRAHME

as Javed Anand says, in the widespread belief that Islam calls for the death penalty for blasphemy and apostasy?[7] Are cartoonists and novelists satanic voices? Have the fear and hatred of the Other truly been overcome in the modern West?

Or does *Fury* represent an attempt to psychoanalytically understand the violence, the "terror" perpetrated in the name of Islam? Are the extremists who perpetrate the violence victims who never want to be victims again? Or are they merely fatherless puppets in unseen hands fucking around with them to create a sort of lust? Thoughtless half-beings full of half knowledge who only know either/or and hate any deeper reflection, who never fight over reasons, not even with the trigger of the Kalashnikov? Misogynistic young men orphaned by a father who could have freed them of their lawless state and given them their duties and their rights, [*Fury* 128] but then died at the right time, so that now they are always in the right—even when they robotically shoot dead people they have been told to shoot dead—by whom?—cartoonists who dared to depict their father? Their Prophet? Their God? And then of course all the Jews anyway, you always have to include that [*Fury* 86] in your list. The willing subjugation of the female perpetrator to an obviously repressive patriarchy leaves the feminist writer-narrator no rational options to explain her behavior. The language begins to take recourse to the comical—not "satire" or "black humor," but a kind of "mockery," of herself as much as of anyone else. It

---

7 Javed Anand, 'The Moderate Muslim Must Address the Reality of Many Lived Islams', *Indian Express*, 6 November 2020. Available at https://bityl.co/CFEp (last accessed on 17 May 2021).

is [l]anguage that grins about itself, so, actually, it is a bitter, mocking laugh (*Three Plays* 545).

Lines begin to blur in the flood of sentences and the ever-changing narrative voices. The deranged ideas of the extremists as *their* voice crows about their time, the coming of the dominance of *their* God alone, when all else is about to be eliminated as *their* God takes over car-rich cities and garbage-filled subways and level streets lined by stores, and when they will have won them all, the fights, [. . .] will have crushed them, the enemies (*Fury* 136)—what exactly is one reading? Is this the delusion of extremists unleashing violence in the name of Islam? Or is this the far-right European politician mongering fear in order to whip up xenophobia and nationalistic passions?

In the translation this becomes more explicit when the French far-right politicians make their appearance and the wordplay extends itself to remind the reader of the sole left-over superpower, nudging them perhaps to think about its role in the senseless violence across large swathes of this planet.

The narrative voice fluctuates between a WE and a THEY and an I—at times the WE are the extremists carrying out the shootings, at times it is a WE representing the urban, urbane, de-provincialized, secularized European wronged by the barbarity of what appears to them as mindless violence perpetrated in blind "Fury." An equally unstable I punctuates the collective narration—at times, it is one of the 'perpetrators' giving the reader a glimpse into a cynicism at the bottom of what appears on the surface to be religio-fanatical violence; at times, it is the apparently reasonable voice of the 'politically active' writer-narrator wanting to but not being able to "believe that one can really intervene" (*Three Plays* 551), fettered as this voice is to the debris of [her] petrified language, which doesn't move, let alone move anyone else (*Fury* 86).

In this fury-induced ruinous daze that our world seems to be trapped in, not only are millions rendered homeless by the endless violence but also the home of our being—our language—is hollowed out, no longer able to mediate the "truth" that it once gave us. Our questions, "reached somebody" who sent us an answer through a chosen messenger. Language, which carried the answer to us, is now inadequate before the power of the truth.

One tumbles along through the text as it rips to shreds all "arguments" in favour of a God over human life, in favour of a religion over human solidarity, arguments that obsess of the elimination the Other for the survival of the Self, implicating thought together with religion as useless— "Religion, in and of itself, is as useless as thinking" (*Fury* 126). And whatever is done in the name of such religion— devoid of human solidarity and love and only for the sake of an unseen absent, absentee landlord of a God—is against everything that still has some kind of rationality (*Fury* 105).

Myth, however, is pervasively present throughout the text. Right from sowing dragon's teeth to idolizing the cult of the hero—who *alone* is capable of transcending the mundane and delivering the good, and the goods—myth and the mythological are propped up and taken down mercilessly to shine a light on the present. The insanity of the cult of heroism is mobilized in the text through the ludicrousness as much as the relevance of comparing acts of violent heroism—the 'mythical' and the 'real'. It brings forth not only the presence of the mythical in the everyday, a visceral archetypal connect, it also makes the horror of the violence contained in those myths palpable again, whether it is Heracles killing his children or, closer home, an Ashwatthama blinded by fury and slaughtering the Pandavas' progeny in their sleep.

Finally, the question remains: what after the *Fury*? When one is done reading the text, are there any pointers to the emergent even as the text emphatically rejects fanaticism and an extreme narcissism engulfed in an unbridgeable Self–Other binary as the most worthless—and dangerous— parts of human consciousness?

Jelinek's texts allow for, and in fact call for a reading on the reader's terms. The uncertain narrator has no definite diagnoses, let alone prescriptions. If questions arise in the reader's mind, the text clearly shows which answers are *not* the right ones. Much in the vein of Brecht's *Wir stehen selbst enttäuscht und sehn betroffen—Den Vorhang zu und alle Fragen offen!*[8] Jelinek's *Fury* leaves questions open. In fact, and here perhaps it is post-Brechtian, it even leaves the act of questioning itself open. It is up to the reader to find both—the questions and the answers—if they want to. Otherwise it is all the same. When everything is dead, it's all the same anyway (*Fury* 158).

---

8 "Disappointed/Disillusioned and moved we see—the curtain closed and all questions open."

FURY

(small epic.
Come on now, Elfi,
That's all you've got?)

Seed? That's what we're supposed to be? Men's seed, no, there are also women, though both sexes harnessed, some just kidnapped, take the two of us and together we're already three. Just a brief reminder, you'll have forgotten all about it by tomorrow and will yell your anger in one direction or another, depending on who you are and what kind of fury is in you and then you will sing your anger, after you've thought about it a bit, for panic is burning everywhere from all the misery that isn't yours. The souls will rise up to heaven, if that's what you believe in, the others will throw themselves to the dogs, all this will be presented over and over again, also today, yes, and also tomorrow, the souls will fly like those doves dispatched by the saint, the seagull swooped right down on them, the hawk does it too, whenever he gets a chance to get to the city. And thus, in your eyes some kind of Will will have been realized as of the day I can't remember, and on another day, which will be the millionth one of embittered strife between two sons having fallen out with each other, yes, this one and that one, and they quarrelled over something, those rulers, nothing to do with rings and princesses, with blond cascading hair and never without my push-up bra. OK, so they can take off more clothes below the belt. Legs and such, they must be seen all the way up to where they join that hair, which is a mystery to me. They are embittered enemies, those rulers, yes, sure, also in that TV series, which thrives on enemies, one more of an enemy, the other less.

Sing the anger, you won't rouse mine with it! So once dragons' teeth were sown and then that seed of men grew from it, something else could have grown just as well, women could have grown there too, for heroes always need them, here, with us, you can see them already, wouldn't they love to dye that man's horrendous head with his own blood, OK, kill him, plain and simple. It's written all over you that this is what you want. So there. So now you kick, no, not like that, differently, you kick ass together with the men's seed, not a bad seed at all, we have to admit. At any rate, when that stuff was thrown there, the men's seeds could not yet be distinguished from the women's, I mean when the seeds where thrown. But immediately they were killing each other, no, not the men the women, men *and* women all the others who were there, first those who were thought to be the progenitors of some other progeny; that won't work here!, all that grows here are our own genies, I mean genes. Or nothing will grow here at all. Those two other tribes over there, they sometimes advance as close as a stone's throw, within rifle range. They might build a city there, several cities, even whole countries, whatever, that's not an option.

Progenitors may not live in the Father-*Reich*, which now belongs to us again. And what belongs to us, we keep. Meaning is emphasis, so whatever we say, consider it emphasized. It helps. So help us all. A victory would have liberated us, we wouldn't have had to pay reparations anymore, instead we would be paid; but Greece, for example, Greece, of course, fails completely in this regard. They don't pay and they will have to pay for it. They will cause their country's demise. And they owe us the most, but they don't want to pay. By winning, we could have liberated ourselves and everyone else. Attack and conquer, that's what it's all about. That's what we'd like to do now. Light, please! We want change for this country, but of course, one should be able to see the change. It's about time. That's what we want. We have a national interest without being nationalistic, we aren't allowed to, and yours truly can be seen in outline already, the young are coming up here and want their future, we will throw our historical reality in their way as a sort of block, you see, something so grand and hard that they can't get ahead, the young, our reality doesn't allow it, we are throwing ourselves in their way and already they are all ready to go, simply because nothing moves, no moving on up, because of the block, they are ready to take us on as the opposition to their struggle, the only kind to spark a people's great spirit and it's on fire already, fire, fire!, yes, a big fire and without fear they aim for the impossible, the children, and the very old are quickly ready to go for a joint leadership with them, it won't be the last harm done to them, I already said so, no, not this time for a change, this time I said something for the first time, it might not happen again. The chairmen agree freedom has a positive resonance, I have the authority to say it here, though not as the first one, that is, I either repeat myself or I copy everything, sometimes it even comes out right, the stuff I copy, pure coincidence, though I can't just yet reach a real agreement with anyone, even if I say one thing at one time and something else at another, so at least I should, like a broken clock, agree with someone at least twice a day. It would really be important to me to describe people, no, to let those speak who strive for the impossible, which is already impossible for me.

We don't want to see the death struggle of these people or other death struggles, but we don't want to see anything else either, we don't want to drag along the bygone any longer, we discard it, as well as the designs for shaping others, we don't need them anymore, we already match our designs, why would we need new ones?, we designed ourselves and here we are, we are our definitive product and this is what we take with us: no bumping us, though no lumping us with others either, no way! We don't need teachers anymore, we are our own teachers, we don't need representatives, we represent ourselves, we don't question anything since we are the answer, we steer ourselves in the right direction, and all those wanting to be leaders, we don't need them anymore, we lead ourselves, we lead ourselves out of an inconspicuous existence into our own creations, we redo ourselves, we are self-created, the thing-in-itself. So let's call ourselves that! Our God? Right here? Not necessary. We say we need him, but we don't, we keep an eye on spiritual guidance, that's where it stays, we lead ourselves, we are leading us on, and on, we are the school that leads us ahead—life itself. Right now we like to watch the death struggles of other peoples who are no longer needed, we like that better and better! And now we are here! We dance wildly around some pillar, I'll tell you later which one, it doesn't matter, it's no longer there anyway; we inflict death struggles on others, their images shall turn to dust, they are already dirt, we don't let ourselves be taught, we always just let others have it. We reject stupid talk, we refuse to be greenhorns, we won't be disabused, but we say we've been dis- and abused and now we strike out.

We spread death struggles, we look into the eyes of children or former children, we hear them calling for father and mother, we hear nothing, we are not their fathers and mothers after all, we close their book once and for all, we extinguish their line, their traces, their thoughts and we put ourselves in their place in this melee of dragons teeth we sprang from, we still have our name, now it's been immortalized, and we are critical, but not inimical, we never kill children, as long as we live. But these children we do kill, because they aren't children anymore. Everything else we can talk about. No, we don't talk, we don't talk about anything anymore, we don't lower ourselves to being underlings. We just lie low and pull the trigger. That's what it's for. But we aim high, and with good reason, for we are mighty. Only those who want to join us building a future spiritual world, we call it spiritual, though it is not, for who still cares about the spirit, who cares about anything but the One and Only one that's true, only those we don't kill, for we, the people defeat you, great God, in virtue, if you are another God. If you are ours you are invincible, that's what we are testing now. And if we kill any, we must have been invincible, exactly. Exactly.

Exactly. Any man defeats any God, who isn't his. We might lack knowledge, since we taught ourselves, we lack data, numbers and whatnot, but what we do not lack is our God, whom we made ourselves. He is the One-and-Only God. There is none besides him. He knew how to slip into us, who sent him to kill children, mothers and fathers, old men, those who call for the father who no longer counts as a man, hasn't counted in a long time, who call for mother, who no longer does us any good?, and now there is no one else but HE. Are they not gripped by fear that the children, all grown, will revenge the clan? We no longer lie down to sleep. We don't hide. We'll save the country whether or not we can be seen. They say we bring about its demise, but no, we save it from ruin and deserve gratitude.

But it's written right here: In fear of the Gods all mankind shall be! Instead, it should say: In fear the Gods of mankind are. But we don't say that, or the Gods won't come at all and what do we do then? Fortunately, they do appear, after we pray, they don't care if the whole city can see them. They befall us like a misfortune. Right there, another one's approaching, what for? No need to be a God just to slaughter, we can do that too. Has he come so that everything feels well, that everything will fit together well and we will be safe? Do we need him for us to be safe where only the birds herald misfortune? Even a God is cautious when he comes to this country. Could it be they'll kill him too? He enters. He came home late from the night without sun, which we'll give Him now, lights on, so that he can be seen, the God, and we get to see something for the film. The house's guardians have long been taken out, he took care of that first thing, our little God. He came as the One and Only God's deputy, to wit the one who won't save us from death. But, in truth he is *the* God, the only one, and he speaks in his own name, which he hardly can write. So he'll just have to say it and press it into the video or how does one say it? He doesn't spare anyone. He films himself as God who brought to light his own monstrosity, the nameless one, no, he does have a name, which he wants to spread now. We live in abundance, which he wants too, his youth adds bite to our lives which are already a bit long in the tooth. He is a brand-new God, what more could anyone be, he goes to where mortals buy all the brands they'd been offered and had ordered, as they had been ordered. Here all men are equal, I tell him and he says, yes, dead on, all the same, and that means dead on the spot. The Jews must always die right away, what more can I say. They followed their Father into this house and, let me tell you, it was the most ill-begotten thing to do. Why do they have to eat? They don't. Why do they buy their food and here, of all places? Why do they follow a word and feel being led by it to the best path? They were led on, for they get murdered. Somebody rushes after them and kills them and shoots a movie about it to boot. That's not an eternal life as promised by another God. They made a wrong turn and it turns out: They don't live for ever.

The ocean roars, the earth shakes, lightning flashes, there is a pain in the chest and then they are dead. They are coming from somewhere, they do their shopping and then they die through our God, the Nameless One. They shall not live. Why not? Because they are what they are; and because their God is what he will be, they must not be, for filled with gold are their dwellings and we? We've got nothing and are wrapped in darkness, but they, the Jews are always in the light. They put themselves there, how else can it be that it's always only they who get to be seen? So we've got to do something. We better do something to be better seen. We

punish people, that's our mission. So now let's punish these
guys here. Never will their fortunes be ours, thus neither
shall they be. We adorn ourselves with their death, like a
ship trailing boats, we are youth trailing death, entailing
death, they won't yield. The Jews don't yield. They should
be gone, but no, they hold on tight. Has danger drawn that
near? That near, it is already here. So the deed gets filmed,
that's looking ahead, the murderer brought one of those
small GoPro cameras, looking ahead, an oracle gave him the
heads up, or does he normally have such a good head that
he thought of bringing a camera? Shooting a video and send-
ing it via the Internet, that works, we can do that anywhere
and to everything, we can shoot those who'd shoot us to
shut us out, that's how we beat them to it, yes, that's what
he did, the young man, the most one can be, a young man,
he did it, technology is no more foreign to him than the fire
to Prometheus, that's what he did, on video and over the
Internet, that that's how it goes, it goes out to the world on
electrons' feet, and it works. He brought the camera, his
youth a small prize for it and he paid an even smaller price
for it—himself— but before him others had paid, three Jews
or four?, who talks about them? Well, I am talking about
them, but not for long, I can't stay, I can't do it well, speaking
that is, and now I can't do it at all anymore, I don't know my
act, I never act, I take a rest, no real misfortune shall reach
me here. What am I saying? I said it too often, how can one
say the unspeakable so many times, as if that would make it
more real? This sad, desolate age of youth, I hate it, only
they can do such a thing! No, I wouldn't want to be young
again, not for anything or they'd have to pay me quite a lot
for being young again! No one will pay me that, no one

would settle for that, as of now I only settle for age, even though I invested a lot in youth, look at that shelf, there is no camera, there is my cream. I want to throw it into the sea, my age, but the sea, that's the name of the cream, won't take it either, that stupid age, neither fish nor fowl, no, flesh, foul flesh?, or rather fish, whatever, and if that won't work, I want to do away with it, youth, which does such horrible things, but it doesn't work, it fights back, nothing works, not even as well as the GoPro camera and he made sure to bring his laptop, this young man of the dark night—who aroused such murderous madness in him? No idea.

Madness and rage and the feet's jumps and the camera's hum, no, they don't hum anymore, they are often built into the cells, but they don't talk, they shoot, they can't be heard but they shoot and they see and they film the feet jumping, the Kalashnikovs' spitting, no one's throwing a rope there, such dark fury! Such dark fury! But woe, everything has been prepared, everything brought along and then that stupid laptop doesn't work. Got it into the supermarket and then it doesn't work! What do we do now? Oh, we don't worry too much! The evil-doer will manage to send the video into the air, across the air and through the air so that everyone will know he beat his way murdering all the way to Charon, the ferryman, one of them has made it, yes, and the film too, sent via the supermarket's computer, already placed on the steps to all editorial offices, not my fault it doesn't get shown. Then the body's building, the action hero's starting place, the starter home gets blown up, it does not fall on any children and he who had murdered before, he, the customers' murderer, the supermarket's customers' murderer, he wasn't sure what he had done there? Surely he was sure, but a film is better, it says more than a thousand words, have I already gone over this limit?, I don't know, I talk and talk, conscious of the murder, yes, the killer will become famous, we will remember his name, I still do, I don't know about next year, I'll remember it until my fury will leave me. And he does it and does it, he takes out his victims like he takes his dogs out, only the former don't come back, the next time, if he is still around he'd have to take out some more, he'd love to, but three, no, four will do too, four pieces is fine and the film-guy will be the fourth, no, the fifth dead, if I counted correctly, did we forget the police woman?, I am afraid we did, yes, and that man also groaned so horribly, I don't know, I have no idea which one it was. His victims moaned, like the bull pierced by the knife or whatever they do with the animals to kill them, blood everywhere, one can smell it, no need to get close to the slaughterhouses, one can smell it for miles, the dead stuff lies in the supermarket, anything dead—get it to me right here! So one can decide in peace and quiet if Jew or not, one has to know that before, surely, one has to be told.

We've got plenty of people, animals not so many, their raising costs money, there are always too many Jews, no matter how many they are, they simply are everywhere, we take care of them, we, their benefactors, we could have also killed them all, but we left some, we can do without them, our fury blows them away, why do they shop? They could also starve to death, they wouldn't have to shop, they wouldn't have to support themselves, we deport them straight to death, they have to settle for that. Thus the deed gets done, but it will only have been done when, yes, when what?, it will have only been done when the filming will have come to an end for good, but the film goes on, the souls flutter from the house of the dead onto the film, no, that's no longer a rescue path, those images are served daily on a small disk, smaller than a saucer, the seize of a small fingernail, why not: a flash-memory, you first have to delete it, like the life you took in a flash, for the drive you'll have to give something back in return, it will only pay off when death has been captured on it for good, for good money, when he burnt himself into it. One always needs proof. Everything must be seen, why else the whole effort? No, you don't have to run! Oh dear God, I say, that must have hurt them a lot!, no, no, it went very quickly, this weapon is highly effective and those images dig themselves in, they won't let go again. Before the deceased could say anything to the city, such as: thank you for taking a shot, no, not with the camera, a shot at taking me in, really inviting me in before something happens, it was already all over.

The apocalyptic steeds are spurred on, foam flies from their teeth, the eagle returns empty after getting rid of its cargo, the fried liver of the Lightbringer, the fiery one, I ate it yesterday, the customers in the supermarket want something else, they just stopped to shop there. Now the shopping has stopped. The Painbringer no longer flies by in a flash, now it's a free fall, the main thing is it's still in a flash, like Icarus, dropped to the ground right on his victims, as if they were one, but they are three plus one, four then. The fifth some other place. Stop hissing like a snake!, it won't bring anyone back to life, refrain from speaking, restrain your eyes from

sparkling, someone might think you are happy about it, be
watchful when someone enters the supermarket again, but
don't rush after him or you'll be the fifth, no, the sixth, I keep
losing track. Couldn't he have put down the victims in a row
for someone to count them? And recount? Of course, you
can also die by your father's hand. If you believe in him it
will happen. The father sent you. The father picks you up
again. Done. Not a beautiful speech, no speech at all. Youth,
the greatest asset, what follows is only despair, which, however, is easier to bear in one's youth. Or no despair at all?
None of this has been caused by despair? There is no despair
around here? Despair doesn't rule here? I don't know. Three
or four Jews dead. After the millions we murdered, it's not
even worth mentioning, neither is the murderer, he does not
mention it either, he records it. So that one can believe it.
He brought everything with him, he took it upon him, he
took out the camera and then he took them all out. Yes, he
also brought the laptop, but it doesn't work, the fighter
doesn't get into the Internet, so there he fights his heart out
and no one will know? That won't do, he only does it so that
everyone can see it, or he won't get into the net that's already
been thrown over him, that's why he doesn't see it, he's stuck
in it but he doesn't get on it, he is the net and he spreads
within it, he can no longer multiply, now or in the future,
the connection doesn't work, those people are dead and have
been recorded, he recorded them, undaunted like an old
man, no, an old man would have to be told, this one was
undeterred and he brought terror into this haunt, no, into
this special supermarket for the pious, who cares, we zoom
in on this house, now it woke up, it didn't work, the connection to the net didn't work, so he used the computer in the

supermarket, it was there already. He sent the film on his memory card via email, but you know that already.

They know it. They were not the recipients, but they know it. Why am I sitting here? Why do I sit here, why do I sit on this trying to get a grip on this, on my self, you already know it all anyway. What am I doing this for? Not to show moderation am I sitting down, in this class I am always made to sit by myself for being a chatterbox, moderation is not my goal and I have not been sent by some lord and master, I would never follow any master anyway, I don't even have one, I descend from the house of night, like the shooter, except that I am always asleep then, I only shoot my mouth off, good thing I didn't see it, when I left it, my sex, in my house. It must have existed, or I wouldn't be here. That's the way it is. The house of Jews must be called on if we don't know whose God is where, so then we call on the Jews and their house, we murder their sons, one, two, three, four, a thousand, it's all the same to us, we smear their blood on the door, we don't use just firstborns for this, we take children, the very old, mothers, uncles, yes, aunts, with pleasure, if they are halfway good-looking; it could prompt us to spare them. Or not. It all depends on us, only on us, the patriots, who even warn the fire not to shoot up so high that it would tower over us. And if we have no fire in our bodies' orifices, like primordial man, who learned to control the world with the help of his holes, by studying the conduct of fire and then either putting it out or imitating it, it all depends, so then, if we have no fire, we'll light some under their asses.

We'll light the fire and throw them in, because us and them, that's like fire and water, belonging together, but not liking each other. And no Goddess, who circumvents us or protects them, those circumsizzlers, where did she go anyway, the Goddess, so we can call her, we'll say, oh Goddess sing the fury, we already said that, hear the fury, it's coming from the car radio, or did we slip a global player into the car?, with music from some other place, sing of the fury of this man, who, set on fire by himself, brought unspeakable horror to these people—well, the Achaens, the ancient ones, OK, not all the old geeks, you can also call them Greeks, whoever they are—who caused unspeakable despair, like our anger which drives us through factories, supermarkets and newsrooms as well as halls producing sons and daughters born in vain and parents soon childless and children soon father- and motherless. That's the kind of lot they are used to. We are the avenging tribunal; if a weak person met us, he wouldn't be around for long. So now let them lament, the mothers and fathers, whoever.

We stopped briefly at our car, because we didn't know where to go, so there are two cars, here's a picture of them blocking the street, I must have misunderstood the picture, like everything else, I don't understand it, but it continues, they are getting into a car, then into another one which they steal, its owner was obviously lucky with his God, or else he wouldn't be around anymore either. Roaring with power or quiet from the effort to pull the trigger—how's that done with a Kalashnikov?, dear gun from the AK family and that doesn't mean the AK Party—google it—hell!, how holy!, this weapon brings misery and relief right after to the shooter, the weapon on its own? Uses part of the energy in the cartridge chamber, no, not from a partridge, let alone Patroclus, who always gets bemoaned, that bundle of energy, no, not from him; so this unit of energy, this part is used to cock the mechanism, preparing it for the next shot that's sure to come. Of course, we practiced it and nothing makes us groan, the weapon screams like a dog whose foot gets stepped on, we pursue our path of power, which is none, that's why it's called power because it's quite a trip whether one has it or not, it makes no difference, killing is necessary, you've got to kill, no matter where the power is, if you want to kill, you can do it too.

Here at this point, fury heats up to a frenzy and the people boil over with anger. The weapon rages now. While the fired cartridge is still in the barrel, a part of the highly compressed gas is conducted into the so-called gas chamber—a practical construction without any other contraptions—where it activates the mechanism that ejects the rejects of humanity, no, the projectiles—as well as the cocking and reloading device, which has to keep going, of course, many would keep going for miles for this outstanding, excellent weapon. Who wants me to fight in single-combat? I fight one against all and this weapon helps a lot, it helps me getting everyone set, there they sit down on the ground and then they fall over sitting, a hero wishes to speak, a film gets shot, the weapon works. Not one pin drops, we wouldn't hear it anyway, no pin, instead the highly compressed gas locked in the gas chamber accumulates the energy to trigger the next shot. And there it comes, limbs rear up like horses, there comes the shot and it's all over and the propellant strikes again, it's just for show, nobody wants to end this strenuous war, on the contrary, it's only just begun, for we drive anyone not driven into a war, the shell moves out, death moves in, the cartridge base hits against the ejector across from the extractor. You should see what an effect that has! It gets itself, the new device gets itself what?, well, what, a new clip, so, the breech bolt takes a new cartridge from the clip and slides it into the chamber, turns and whoosh!, the studs lock into the slits in the barrel bolt that connects the barrel and the system box thus locking the bolt. The cartridge is held in and then no longer, then it is released, finally it is released! And what a relief it is!

I am not going to tell you in what position the weapon is on safety and when it isn't. Not now, safety catch! Now nobody is safe anymore. Safety catch on, loading no longer possible. Here you can pause briefly, just for loading and then you must promptly continue to shoot. Much is endured on account of this weapon, I might say and so can many others. You see, it's not about sleeping through the night, many images pop up then and enter our heads and then there's no mercy, that's the principle of those people, no one shows any mercy. We bring ruin, but we say that was sent by God. That's our secret, which we yell out at every opportunity. That's no secret. If I hadn't said it, I wouldn't believe it myself.

So there they're wheezing or not, all is all or not, it's all like that or not or no different or different. So they're breathing out their last souls, whose arms beat against their body against the cold or not, snorting, moaning, screaming or saying nothing, woe, sigh, her flower is broken, oh city, you won't be able to extinguish this anymore. Three are falling there and a forth in another room along with others, everything's falling, that watch too, no, that hand, everything falls at once, that can't end well, there should have been the sounds of dance and play, but those didn't want to today. Today only death has been available, death is the special of the day today, so everything's for nothing today, everything's always for nothing anyway, except death; it costs you your life, but today it's free for all. The bringers of woe race away in a car, then in another, Gorgons of the night, no, it's broad daylight or people would not be shopping and drawing, enough!, flight in a compact, or was it midsize? At any rate, they are shooting off, goading the engine, faster, we've got a job to do, we also know how to, but it's not done yet, so we Gorgons are speeding away, we'll be here in a moment, a print shop in the suburbs, the school next to it, there we can't cull the children, quick, go, everything's gotta go, with the hissing of snakes and the spitting heads of the weapons, with sparkling eyes and the hundred heads with only waste inside them, we stuffed our heads with waste to keep them straight or we wouldn't be able to see where we are shooting, the heads have to remain straight on top, our Gorgon heads turned forward, we keep watch, a hundredfold, no, only threefold, that'll do, two here, one over there, a Gorgon with his head full of shit held up high, but what we know, what we know for sure, what we know exactly and all the others don't know, so then what we know is that we, like a God, hurl those unfortunate ones down to their own God and they'll die quickly at the hands of us.

Oh miserable us! But now I don't know who'd be so miserable that he'd do such a thing. There we knock them off, and
there they lay, all good, the earth below, the sky above, which
they don't see anymore, they only see the shelves in the
supermarket stacked for them, but no longer in their bags,
they won't be filling their bags at our expense any longer,
the merchandise stays on the shelf, there are only four customers less on the premises. And a piece of brave soul, hello,
whose is it, it just lost its master, but we don't believe in
souls, we believe in our weapons, yes, the killers are always
interesting, aren't they?, everybody knows their names. I
don't know the names of the Jews, maybe they didn't want
their names to be known, though, on the contrary, if the
names get erased, the people get erased. Their names should
not be lost, can you please tell me where I can find these
names, where are they written down, I lost them, though it
could be that I never had them, never known, never mentioned, never shown on television, never trending on the
streaming services, low tide, high tide, waves come and go,
right now they happen to be gone, most of the time they
just come and end up in us, the streams, streams of knowledge, so, there I said it and I repeat, and many brave sons of
heroes, here two pieces, one piece there, and here too,
another piece, no, not another piece, this here is not a piece,
not a dramatic piece, won't become one either, millions of
pieces, all gone, all gone, three more still, really now, that
one wouldn't have been absolutely necessary, nevertheless,
it was conditionally necessary, the presence of the victims
conditioned the killers, so that those others, just by going
shopping already present themselves to be robbed by the
dogs. And look, already the murderer guided his foot to the

winged words of his God and his proph, his prof; the killer, who never has the blood of the dove, no, the real spirit streaming into him, he is completely sober, in contrast to all the others, that one doesn't slip on the blood he got out of other people, blood for blood, his follows later, the helmeted ones will take him out, those helmeted ones with their vests and shields, the iron-, no, dough-armoured ones, nothing goes through that, not even the shot from the Kali and that's how it should be, sleep no more, death to all, at least as many as possible, first these, then those others.

OK, that won't make the house break down, only those inside fall victim to the horrible oath they won't break, which they swore to their God, whose name they shout, roar, can't do without, without ever taking the holy name of their God in vain, not their own will that led them to it, it was their God, who is great, or was it their will after all?, the gatherer of black clouds who is always right, as much as I know, at least that's what he believes. My God is the greatest, he says, the name of the others' God bleeds out of their mouths, maybe they wanted to position theirs?, but the others' weapon was already at the ready and the attack succeeded, it is horrific, now some are going to the host of their immortal Gods. They'll be surprised when they don't find them, because they don't exist. So much work and then they don't even exist! I wouldn't want to be in those murderers' skin, then again not in mine either, but I apologize, that doesn't count here, here we are counting the perpetrators and the victims, neatly separated, no question. My hand shall fall off, if I did not speak the truth and how am I supposed to continue to write then?

The biggest and most horrendous oath to their God drove them here, now it can't be undone anymore, there's no key for that, even though they always carry their electronic junk with them, which can't be deleted. Those people have been wiped out and no return key, no revert key will bring them back. They have an earth-shaking king, a God, whom they are doing it for, but where is he, where is his holy head to which a false oath is sworn, one every second, and the God accepts it too? What God accepts such an oath? I advise you not to do it, not to take an oath, but you still do, take something else, but no one asks me. I speak, my God smiles or he doesn't, because I don't have one. They, however go to their God, which is an entire host, a club of more than seven hundred, because one single one could never manage that kind of global enterprise, that's who they pray to five times a day or more often, they call him, they throw themselves into the carpet pile and then they armour themselves like the Greeks, who wised up in the meantime. They can't armour themselves, they are left with nothing. Well, no, they still have tanks.

Exactly. Now they finally got started, armies in armoured vehicles, they spent a lot for these tanks, the Kalashnikov was comparatively cheap, yes and they have started it already, don't ask me who!, they have left their house already, they are already on their way to an editorial office and a supermarket and a print shop, the latter no longer a voluntary visit, the mosque yes, they visited like the rulers of the sea, just without sea, like the rulers of the land, just without land, instead they are ruled by their God, he is in charge, yes, so they walk into a newsroom and into that supermarket, where they kill Jews and they don't enter any palaces because they aren't let in there, they don't get in there, they are angry, they are furious, they explode over nothing and can't extinguish the fire burning inside them with water anymore, no flame to warn them to stay small the way they are, to stay small and stop twisting like that, whatever, they'll find them, those top gunners, it's just a matter of time. And now time has run out, the fire died down, the dead are mourned by the other dead who are already high up on Mount Olympus, the heads of state minus the one of America, but he says he's also mourning mightily along with them.

The victims have been delivered. Smartly, the doctors remove the flesh from the bones. Who'd know their names, oh yes, the names of the cartoonists, those are known. I just hear that Zeus, also a God, if yours exists, why shouldn't Zeus still exist too?, well then, Zeus was really POed, that his victim, that is the one sacrificed to him, consisted only of fat and bones, the nerve of it!, what's with the flesh, where's the beef? The real thing! Where is it? The Gods always want to get to the core and let humans get there too, and then there is nothing but a few measly bones, pelt, skin, a stomach nobody wants or needs. The God's fury is frightful, and this is why the murderers are mourning, their God is furious that not all people belong to him, but only a few shreds of pelt, skin and a few pieces of bone, hacked, one can't even tell what that used to be, one can't even see what animal it was, maybe it was a human, who had been sacrificed. And the butchers are approaching already, they'll take care of it all.

And could there be one among them who'll just bite, that one, a dog who shot a movie about the murder, looking ahead, and also his screwing earlier, I don't know, but there must have been some, a while ago, for the shooter's wife, the veiled image at Sais, had already been led away from somewhere to something, taken by handlers into the battle, into the war, she is well there, it serves her right there, what did I want to say, such is the will of God whom I can't name, the will I can, but not the God, what about the PR effect?, if the God can't first be announced by name then the killing's no longer worth it, then people won't know who, when and what for, thus the will of God is to be named and not named at the same time, maybe he is to be named indirectly, who knows, his name is written everywhere, and what's written can also be wiped out or they take themselves out, but they won't go away, they'll pull it off, they'll pull the trigger, they'll just do their thing. Thus the will of that one's been done and the wife is with Nobody, the veiled picture has been brought to the other pictures, which are also veiled, how is one to know what's behind it all?, she is nobody, the wife, she doesn't want to be anybody, she wants to be invisible, I am everything that is, has been and will have been. No mortal ever lifted my veil and no one should ever dare. She crosses the border, she is led across the border, she still saw great rage against her husband incensing the hearts, flowers are laid down where the dead had been, I am saying it again and I say it to the veiled picture of a woman, who, nevertheless has also been shown in just a bikini in pictures on the other page, I swear, surely, you must have also seen those some time, I say it again, maybe not for the last time, but this time I am telling her, we even know her name and we know her face from the bikini pix, and I am also telling her: The Gods are a Nothing. And that means all of them. Yes, yours too. All of them. And humans are great, but she knows that, she knows that anyway. Or doesn't she after all? Sweet children's lives were simply thrown down by those men, like for a final sale, everything must go, lives are chucked, and my great rage is directed at them, yes, Hera rages, I rage, they should not have been able to do that. I know their names, I know the name that's behind the veiled picture, and that name, those names shall know that I'll be raging against them as long as I live, well, who am I?, still, I'll do that and I can also be terrible any time, even if not a Goddess, but I am terrible in my rage, which does not effect anything, yep!, maybe there will be a revolution, not today, but some time and then everyone will know that the Gods are Nothings, great though are humans if their murders are not atoned for. What am I talking about here? I usually know, this time I don't. Haven't they been punished already, aren't they dead too, OK, for whenever I punish somebody it doesn't work, I tried it with mom, result: flop, it's not a pleasure, only writing is a pleasure for me, but that doesn't punish anyone. Well, I still don't know the names of the victims, only the names of the famous, the celebs, those I know, that's how it always is. I don't know who died in that supermarché, I don't know them, someone must know them. How can I write them down here when I probably don't know, no, certainly never knew them? So then, I am everything that ever was and ever will be. No, I am not. And I won't ever be. Once is enough.

Those stupid Gods, divided by bitter quarrels, therefore two pieces of Gods, at the very least and now they are fighting each other to the bone and those bones they'll shoot as well, those bullets go through them like a hot knife through butter, like a hot panty through a man's brain, I beg your pardon, I am sure that this is not how it works. So those two had a fall-out, the ruler of one people and the ruler of the other, and now we have to pay for it, no, we don't. With the Kalashnikov the spring sustains the tension, which I, unfortunately cannot sustain, so that it has enough energy for one shot or continuous shooting, I immediately pick one image, not a veiled one, a real one, so I get to know it better, with the Kalashnikov it is the charge that does it. Those who got killed have to pay for it. Always the others. Not us. Not us. We, however, avoiding extinction, join our comrades. Something flies over us noisily. Was this already the vulture to get the liver?, half a pound liver please, I'll cut it myself, only I know how I like it, only I can do it, dear God, my old tune won't help me here, and the divine education won't help me either, probably because I haven't got it, but that's not what I wanted to say, the others are cowards, the enemies are always cowards—just letting themselves be shot, three people, no, four, and it gets filmed to boot, they probably filmed the vulture too, who flew in to get his liver diet, beautiful nature shots, the way he flies across the landscape, always seen from below, of course. Most people see everything only from below. People are cowards, they went shopping unarmed, that's why they have to die, they are always unarmed when they have to die, except when they armed themselves, that also happens, I'll be happy to tell you where they are armed, don't go there, I'd advise you, but I don't say it, I say tons of words, but in fact, I am not saying them or you'd dress me in stones because of the tragedy that I, of all people! have allegedly caused! The vulture take it! Yes, the eagle can take it too. Greedy beast, always has to shred liver, but first he has to get it, at the supermarché of all places and the next day he is coming back again, the bird, who feels like eating, over and over again and again, no, not the next day, that's when the market is closed; the day after next it's open again, then whole flocks of birds are coming, screaming, the eagle hides among them, but you recognize him easily, you already recognize him by his size, sailing, shooting through the air, is someone shooting here?, did someone shoot and finish off four?, I don't think so, no, it is the griffin shooting down, he does not offer a deadly attack like the Kalashnikov, he wouldn't be able to, for his victim can't move, it is forged to the rock, it does not resist. I inhale war courage and then I exhale it again and again.

Brief interlude with vulture, no, eagle, so that they can recover a bit, those four on the ground, they won't run away from you anymore, let them lie there, let's take a look what that eager bird is doing with the liver, though it really doesn't interest me all that much. It is remarkable though that love and fire are always mentioned together, so then the fire starts and many get aroused by it, no question. And, believe it or not, the flame suggests in color and form, no, in the twitching of flames the arousal of the vigorously active penis. Back then it was still productive, the fire of passion was still active, the fire's tongues active still, everything highly active. Back then people were still really working! Is that the eagle over there, with his fated little package, baggage every one of us must carry every day? No, it isn't. The consumption and renewal of that stupid liver, what is it telling us? It is a constant up and down, the bird keeps returning every single day to sate itself, yes, and lust, the lust for love, not to be confused with the lust for life, though both won't do you any good, well, it gets its daily satisfaction in order to daily restore itself again. Like the sun. That pecker, right?, it goes limp for a while, fill in here for how long, but no cheating!, sit down, relax and look at yours, I can't do that, I don't have one, take the time to get together with yourself, are you relaxed?, for yourself and others, write it down, I know you'll lie, but after a while, it could be a whole day or longer, it goes limp and will be revived anew. Like the sun. That's nice, isn't it? Nice thought, right? Execution more difficult. The chewed through liver of the Fire-bringer, not of the undertaker, he brings the fire to others in case they don't want a six-feet-under, right?, I mean the eagle, who devours the liver, every day anew, that's whom I mean, you can set your clock to it, that means, well?, what?, that means the restoration of our dreadful, dreary, evil desires for their termination through satiation, that is their indestructibility, humans are easily destroyed but not their lusts, they shall remain intact, for ever and ever.

Here you have a photo of it, but you won't get anything out of it. Destroy and restore, for ever, that would be it, for the eagle does not abstain, there isn't a single day his drive gets offended and yours won't have to either, it doesn't have to get hurt either. Your drive to fuck and to kill, as the case may be, is recallable any time, but only if you are lucky, it's of no use to me, because my drive can't be seen, many have told me so, it must be located somewhere inside, actually, this isn't what I wanted say, I didn't want to insert myself here, in fact, I was strictly forbidden to do so, I beg your pardon, Wolfi, just one more time, so then, primordial man's drives must not get insulted, that's what I want to get at together with the thinker because, unfortunately, I can't think on my own, that's what I want to get at, the pecker wants to come out and then he can't find anything there, the liver has been eaten for today, there he flies already, the eagle, he is flying home again, but he'll come back tomorrow, don't cry!, don't cry for the dead!, I think they don't even want that, the dead, it's a narcissistic insult to them. Only those tears confirm and certify their death. So we are also treating the negation of drives, but that one isn't treatable or negotiable, negation is not an option, no negation and no penalization, the attacker is dead too anyway, right, and now Freud Sigi falls off his rocker, as the perpetrator's punishment is followed by the assurance that in fact he did not effect anything, the perp, go ahead, you can pass this on to him, I don't mind, I don't always have to do this myself. But the murderer won't hear you, he passed on too. I could say a lot more, but I practice denial, not so the eagle, he flies off with his liver and then he will be killed, how is that possible? Killed by a Heracles, earlier he had smothered the serpents' licking tongues so that you won't be afraid but take a close look instead—he smothered the flames, those flames that kept growing back just like the liver of that Fireman, everything's working, when my dog had taken our home apart, my insane father said those words: He worked hard today, so he also must eat well and so he did. Those who work must also eat, but also the others, what's gone out keeps growing back

again, but not everything, that's what I am trying to get at
but cannot say, example: the flames grow back as long as
they get fed, the murderers grow back as long as they get
dispatched, they look into a small man-made device—made
under difficult conditions—and they deliver, and they know
everything that can be done with fire, and the liver of the
Fireman—not to be confused with the firefighter—also
keeps growing back as long as it is always taken away from
him, yes, exactly, you already know about the eagle, the liver
grows back as long as it gets taken, hacked off, pecked off,
that long it will also grow back again and again. If the liver
stayed where it was, it wouldn't have to grow back again,
then everything would come to a standstill. If people would-
n't always grow back, the killing would come to a dead stop,
all killing would come to an end, if people were thus finally
coming to an end as well no one would have to pull the cock,
I mean, cock the gun and pull the trigger, or draw the shit
card and stare at the gurgling foaming water, oh fuck it, what
gets restored is always only the destruction.

I don't know how it goes. But there are the dead no one can
awaken. And there that eagle keeps flying for his deliciously
roasted liver, first liver, flames later, dish done and gone, but
not for good, since it must be eaten over and over again, we
are dealing here with a barbecue that goes on out of doors,
free and easy, in a land of the free, that's where the liver gets
grilled every day, the eagle could have opened a restaurant
long ago. The Fire-bringer wants to maintain the fire, even
though his liver gets stolen by a bird over and over again,
bye-bye birdie, the fire guy wants to see his work—the
fire he fetched with great effort, preserved, but the bird's

murderer lets the fire collapse, at this point I don't see where the fire came from and where it is going. What does Freud mean by it? No idea what fire he means, but I'll look it up. I am so tired, and those guys are still killing themselves and I am still so tired. Freud thinks that one can't piss and procreate at the same time, every man knows that. Those two can't be brought together, they are like fire and water, they are fire and water, they have to decide right now, they don't get a grace period: Do you want to produce water or do you want to procreate, just so that some other guy will take out the offspring again? The water extinguishes the pecker and his lust. You can't have them both together. You've got to decide, extinguish or open fire! Man, yes, it's true, man extinguishes his own fire with his own water. That's something no one should let pass, it is a fundamental choice. And he who kills, extinguishes. That's what I say. So, now I said it.

The Gods are a Nothing and great are only humans. Tell that to the filmmaker who'll be dead in a moment with all his gifts, which will die with him, and take a few people along as provisions, no, no idea if that one was gifted! He wouldn't have believed you. With all those people being so small when they get into his camera. Rulers, please look into the device, into the lens, please look: meaning, here's the bird coming out, here comes the vulture, why am I always thinking vulture?, it is an eagle!, totally different stuff of bird!, so that's what's coming out, interesting!, the one who'll devour the liver, the birdie, that's where you have to look, that's where the birdie's coming out, I already said it, I am always saying everything at least three times, no, more often, but four dead are still lying here too, the fifth some other place, wasn't that the police woman or another dead woman, for every one of my words one plus two more, or two plus two, the vulture take it, they are all dead, I already told him several times these words are meant for him, they are for this bird, and he actually does it! He comes and gets them! He even does what he is told! And the rulers turn their blessing eyes away from all that (be)getting, well, this one in any case, faces are turned away, but not fate. It's not their fault. Faces are turning away, fates don't get turned away, except this one, which I won't mention here and as for the grandson, yes, this one and that one too, I don't have any, the ancestor's once beloved, quietly speaking features are not seen, simply not looked at and not seen, so why grandchildren, whatever for? No recognizable connection, we wouldn't know with what.

We did not foresee that, no, that one would no longer be able to see where one came from and therefore creates something new and that then is what one must be. Thus speaks this movie, I haven't seen it yet and I won't watch it either, I am not going to that movie house; I didn't see the murder, the murders, I saw nothing, even though it would have been possible, easily with a little effort, it'll show up on my screen, but I will resist this new beginning, I don't want to see it, I don't want to see how someone takes on the responsibility, who had ceded all responsibility to the caliph long ago. Good for him. Bad for the victims. Therefore, my words will say something entirely different but in what way I can't yet say either. The man that addresses us that way has no more responsibility, but we are supposed to have it? He proceeds against everybody just for a bigger effect? If all were dead, it would have the biggest effect, but who would

admire him then?, no one left, no one around for the brave
men's fight, but preferably against those who are not brave,
they are easier to deal with, they stand by our side, not opposite us, that won't bring shame, it won't bring dishonor, it
will be our victory, only no one will see it anymore. What
battle heroes have we kidnapped here, who unfortunately
are no longer at our command? Every geezer in his bed
understands that: You attack us, we attack you. Even I get
it. I can't bang out a simpler sentence: Bang-bang-bingo. The
weapon is still safely locked, soon it will be cocked and the
body, please pick one, all of them, that is all you can see here,
not the others of course, are at your disposal, so just take
the one who happens to be around, who is nearest to you
and over there are a few others who raise their frightened
eyes up to you, oh, that's good, your son will thank you for
this, the victim's son certainly not. Try getting through that!
That one will need help, and help will be offered to him.
Well, the body is ready for hardship, and the trigger mechanism is set for absolute safety, no, not on safety, the weapon
can't be on safety, it wouldn't function that way. Cock and
fire, that's all there is to shoot for and that doesn't just go
for the one with his hand on the cock, it's coming from his
caliph, it's a herculean job we execute for the caliph here,
people should be thankful for it, but who's thankful anyway.
There are no thanks for such a thing. So there the hero
purified land and sea, mastered enormous toil and trouble,
created heaven and earth or whatever it was their God
accomplished, I don't even want to know it, he did terrible
things, oh please, I don't want to hear it, let alone say it, I
stuff my ears and close my eyes, I don't need any special aids
for that, the hero has cleansed so many, sawed off heads,

burned one guy in a cage, so that the crap can stay in one place and be removed, so that the wind won't carry it off, for the show must go on, others it drowned, a real show-stopper, that wind, so let's get them here in time! The cameras are very small and transportable, they are coming with us wherever we go, yes, that's what he did, that's what those heroes did, they drove there and just did it and how are they thanked? Accused, what did you do to all those people, all those passengers you transported, talk! I wanted to emigrate so I can live there peacefully according to Islamic rules, which are the only true ones. And you, the second accused? I only wanted to get a ride to a vacation, I wanted to splash around in the Black Sea and instead of booking a holiday package I got into the taxi arranged by acquaintances and calculated expenses between only 100–150 euros one way. And, accused, what are those pictures on your smartphone, pictures of the black flag and fighters, doing there? They aren't doing anything there, they are stuck. It has something to do with my membership in a chat group, I received these files unwantedly and have nothing to do with them.

Nevertheless, their gaze does not search for a weak enemy, no, rather a strong one, but that one's not here, out of town for an indefinite time, as far away as possible, certainly not to where the battles are, but yes, of course!, there too!, we'll go there, you bet, tickets have already been taken care of. But until we get there, we'll take anyone for an enemy, who happens to be around, we aren't picky that way, we don't mind destroying the weak, if there are no strong ones at the time, hey, you, the gaze is looking for you who have nothing but an empty mouth with a tongue in it which gives off sounds and it can't even do that, it needs vocal cords for that and also a few other things, a much more complicated mechanism than a Kalashnikov, man is not built in a simple way, he's a very complicated construction, if he had done it himself, it would have been much simpler, so that the murderers would have it easier with him, so many mechanisms have to be silenced, immobilized, now please!, all of this is work, well, not for us, the machine does it for us, luckily we have it, our arms' strength is leaving us, but this gun keeps its power, it stores it in a gas chamber, you already know it, with highly compressed gasses carried into it, where they hit the gas piston, proven a million times in all the chambers which were built for that purpose, and that reverts the gas piston in its guide tube, can you imagine! Look, like this! Because of this incredible force carried forward everything's going to come out, nothing will come out, because everything has already come out, we shaved after ten years of facial hair, why?, to take a three-week vacation at Bulgaria's shores, that's where we tan seamlessly, also in the face, this machine, however, doesn't know that, but this machine is not aiming at us. In short, no, not short: the whole process of cartridge case ejection, cocking, reloading and during automatic gun fire—I am not sure now about the fire, or am I?—well, during the new firing process, during the automatic shooting process, you've got to press the trigger only once, right, and the whole thing comes out, it gets shot out, the bullet, surely it needs to know where to, doesn't it?, so you have to be told, and now you know it.

You can forget the rest, the rest can't even forget anymore, it doesn't know anything and doesn't learn anything anymore either. Let's talk about what divides us. Yes, let's talk, that would be better, it would be better if we talked to each other, can't call this talking, just tell me why you want to kill those people! What did they do to you, talk! You kill us, we kill you, that's really a very simple answer. We kill you, because you are the ones who decide what is to happen everywhere on earth! But here you do not decide, here you certainly are not the deciders! That doesn't convince me, so then, what is it? What did these victims do to you? We can't imagine that you are afraid of them, so what did they do, these victims, what did they do to you? You being afraid?, we don't buy that, we don't buy anything, you better keep that to yourself, that's your problem. Why should we, because you are too cowardly to fight against armed men, why do we have to die, we didn't do anything? So here you demand to be the master over this country, you athletic young fellows as you refer to yourselves vis-a-vis the beautiful young women or—even better—virgins who come to pray to you, no, to your God, they don't know who is who, that's good, and paradise is a perfume section in the department store, where everything you want comes as a gift to you, that's paradise, every color's up for grabs there and then it comes with you voluntarily. Unfortunately, we still have to pull the veil over it and are not allowed to lift it.

How come that among those wimps, those douchebags, among those thousands of millions of men, there aren't many to defend yours? Well, I don't know either. I don't really know. What? I don't know. The exiled are listening in night-dark caves. Someone's shaking his head, is it I?, No, that's not I. I have no children, no grandchildren, I have no

one and I just shake my head, because I can't think of anything else. Whoever did it should come forward right now, it
doesn't have to be to me, but he better come forward after
all his bragging about it. Have him prove it. The proof will
be delivered not orally, not in writing, but right away as an
instant image, as a practical image pack which can run
instantly, which can instantly start running again, or however
the electron does it, great job, electron!, whatever can be
delivered will be delivered and that'll be the end of it. It'll all
be delivered and everybody will have had it. Everything will
be delivered upon request or without it as an image, that's
what we want. We want an image that brings no thorns into
the bed of roses we lay down in. And it is not permitted to
do evil, that's why we don't do it or only reluctantly.

We took care of this house, we opened it up and now the
door won't close again, the door, which we closed ourselves,
the one to the father's house. We hold on to our power with
eternal hands, and with the other hands, so many hands that
are coming to help with murder, we hold it shut. They push
against it from the outside, no idea who, but that won't help
them to live longer, no one can wield power at will, but they
all do it nonetheless. He steals the power, and so then he just
has it. And he whom we uplift, that man fears it double, the
power, there he is, the one lifted, on cliffs and on clouds the
corpses are prepared for him around golden tables as well
as escape vehicles and empty factories with lockers and
supermarkets with cold stores, where they hide from us, the
cooling is turned off by a good person, with whom hostility
could not prevail, yes. Welcome to the cold room, dear
guests, before they come, this cooling will just have to be

turned off, all done!, thanks, welcome all, disgraced and dis-
honored, as you happen to be, but still in the deep dark
chasms of your God whom we don't acknowledge, we've
got our own, thank you much, who includes only us, whom
we, however, don't know at all. Who, in turn, is not acknowl-
edged by others. And so it goes for all eternity.

Fettered in darkness, you are waiting in vain for a just judge-
ment, just is only ours, it is the last one and is still valid. And
that means for all! Only our God is just. You have none, you,
however, you are against ours! Says who? Who said that just
now? I won't mind to kill a whole city, and upset the enemies' swarms until they'll come after me which, however,
won't do them any good, I ask: Who was it? Who got
secretly into the country and turned off this cooling? The
people could have died back there without us having to work
for it, well not us, of course not, only one did the killing and
filming and he would do it again, but that wouldn't have
been necessary. Who turned off the cooling so that you
wouldn't freeze to death? This gentleman here, called res-
cuer for short, many thanks, please step up to the micro-
phone. No one could force him into the fight. Why not? Well
now, you can't really do that with everyone. He was hiding
you and turned off the cooling, so you wouldn't have to die,
simple as that. There they kneel—others, soon their heads
will be off, mercy! Add mercy to mercy, they scream, we
implore all of you, that you, the One and Only, help us, whoever you are. Please listen, please let up, please look at eye-
level, not below, nothing to see down below, for the eyes are
above, he who has eyes to see shall see, if he wants it so
badly, I cannot look at this. I can't bear it. Let others bear it,

I won't. They are to be beheaded, and one, I already said it, trembling, what if they catch me too, one was burnt alive, who'd do such a thing!, we haven't done it in a long time, I can't even bear an image of it, which I've made of it, but with no talent, I bear my father's name, the name of the son of a son, none of them had murdered, even though he could have been easily murdered when the city was still smouldering with the fire of conviction and excitement and steaming from the extinguishing water, it was all designed that way, if I am not all mistaken, but sadly I am. Everyone misleads me. I request from my ancestor, that all this must end right now. But it doesn't. Nothing ends, everything remains, even though everyone is dead. Well, that's no comfort to me. One burning here, others getting their heads chopped off there. I repeat myself: The Queen's delicate foot, come on now, Elfi!, so what?!, no one cares, the foot comes to a halt. That's still the way it is, no matter how often I write it down. Those shot were filmed as they got shot, so people would know that no misdeed ever dies. So here it's running, the film or whatever that's called now and now it has run out, as quickly as the time it has taken. They are sitting somewhere, who-ever, including the mother or whoever's still alive hoping that those children don't suffer death and there they die. The thought's hardly finished and they are finished. We can't even guard this site, for it was in a film, it passed too quickly for us to stand in front of it. Cut off we sit in our own house, at a loss.

I couldn't picture it, no wonder. Paint me that picture on the walls of my grave, then I'll no longer have to look at it. He doesn't work miracles their God, that One and Only, who shall never favor us, so they say, always only the murderers, who still don't know him either, as little as anyone can know his God, he only knows his own, but not his God, so, yes, he has an appeal but its effects are appalling, he doesn't effect anything, at least not with me. All I know about him is that he exists. No one knows him, how could he, who should know him, who would know anything. The self-made is easy to recognize, because almost always it is poorly made, professionals can do it better, but they don't have as much fun with it. But with this God I can't tell if he is home-made or bought. He doesn't seem perfect to me, that takes some more practice. Perhaps raise the temperature somewhat? Sharpen the whittle? Sharpen the pencil? There, that shuttered house, it must be searched. And that one too and there's another one. This God is self-rolled and self-stuck in the mouth and he also goes up in smoke before he gets to deliver. And just the amount of knowledge and the miles of statues that must be destroyed for him to come are enormous. He seems to need more square meters than St Peter's, more space than then the Orion spacecraft to Mars, yes, exactly, enormous, a word which I think I never used. And it has only been lent to me. Enormous. The suffocation of any original and consistent desire to know must be executed as does the sabotage of any attempt to unfold a rational existence. We don't need any of it anymore. Now we don't need it anymore. Heidegger might have still needed the mind and he believed that others needed it too, well, I don't need it. I have enough with what I always said: We must die, I and you, just like those people there, if not as horrifically with fire and knives and Kalashnikovs and such, all that stuff about sheltering breasts I can do without. Mommy is dead.

Who says so? I do. And with gratitude. But those guys are saying, those father- and motherless ones are saying, mother, where, oh where has father gone? Dead. Father, where, oh where has mother gone. Dead too. Dispersed. Don't know. But we are not surprised that even they have fled before us, since we know neither father nor mother. Who could have comforted us with words, they don't exist anymore. When the door creaks, we oil its hinges, we enter, we dispatch everyone; prostrating ourselves before a father's precious knee is not what we do—there is no father, only God, our Lord, who is so big that we cannot look beyond him. Thus, we can be sure he is looking out for us. Looking down on us. What hope can he impart to us? None, that's not his job. We put an end to *being*, as long as it isn't ours, others are doing that for us, but then everything must really have ended. It must be all over. Nothing must be opened. Every-thing must be shut close. Mass rapture must erupt, where purely physical masculinity morphs into the brutality of heroism, that's possible, yes, it works with a Kalashnikov, all of it can be done with one and two flame throwers and a rocket launcher and an anti-tank missile and a cage, where the burning can take place, or an atomic bomb, everything can be done much more efficiently with an atomic bomb. That rapture—how do we kill this one now and that one there?, whom do we kill until we can no longer count the enemies and simply kill them all, that way we gain time until new ones are coming, for they all are our enemies until even more powerless are coming, who must not get the time to save themselves, no, and they don't get a place for it either when death is close to them, their only relative, so let him come, for never shall weary humankind's woe, we'll take care of it all right; the wind breathes, yes, it breathes too, it must inhale sometimes so that it can exhale, we're not the only ones who do it, the wind breathes gently or it blows on us vehemently and we fall, we have plenty of room, all others have been cleared away, all others are already gone, everything, everything keeps changing, nothing stays as is. That's very good for the community, that's why we swagger in constant rapture but now we have ourselves in control, luckily, let the sinner lose heart, we, the slayers won't let up.

As of right now, this mass rapture qualifies as communality and this community of believers who don't have to believe at all, they must not believe in common sense and they have to be uncommonly monstrous, right?, and they have to be very many, right?, a true community that is, which, however, could already be attained with just a few, I would call so many an overkill and this will then be passed off as the common ground for everything else, that community, here, shoulder to shoulder, there, at the counter, right there, jobs and grounds, legal or not, will be plotted out, in case you need one, draw a number!, here they have plots for everything, where is there space left for anyone doing anything himself, making it big on his own, establishing himself, effecting change, for example, in this Europe, that's right around the corner, that's the place where the doors get shut close to every refugee, that is everyone who could get away and get here, yes, go ahead, you can say it out loud: So what are we still living for, they don't exist anymore either, are they?!, where are Europe's friends?, here's one, but he's not enough, I am not enough, time to get ready for death, what are you waiting for?! You want to live forever? What's going to save you? Oh, but no, there won't be any room. No room left anywhere, not even in the storage room. Only the room for God, that one we'll spare, we won't spare that one for ourselves, we can spare ourselves that one, the room, not the God. For everything belongs to him, we too, we belong to him. He, however, the One, he stays at his everlasting feast. He won't drop in, today he's got no time for that, but now we have some more time again—we already brought out the weapons—, to rise like hawks, the weapons will help us, I hope. Our locks turn red, I have to dye mine myself and those aren't locks. I stare into the box with the raging images. If that pack will burn, if they'll burn everything, that's not OK with me. I tell them: I am the Lord of this city, not your Lord, that's not a Lord at all the way he behaves, I am not the dead one there, I am the other Lord, who still can do something, if not for long maybe. Yes, do not bewail me, better bewail your lot, learn to cower before the power of this Lord, we would call him Lord God, who committed horrific bloody deeds and has more of them still in preparation, but those are also almost ripe! To urgently warn about a religion we shall speak, but it is not enough. We blame everything on this God who is represented by people in Toyota pick-ups, the majority of whom certainly does not consist of peace-loving creatures and I don't mean these cars, of course. We'll see soon enough what they have in mind for us and I don't mean these cars, of course. They'll give birth to even more extremists, well, yes, their women, won't they? Harness them to this carriage and I don't mean those women, of course. They race away like bloody horses, who had come to the bloody trough and voraciously crunched human carcasses, I don't mean the horses, of course, I only mean their horse powers. And all, all, all of them rejoice in this cannibalistic meal. Now he actually brings in the harvest, now they are serving it up, after he had promised it for years, the lord and master, I don't mean that master, of course, I don't even know who that is. All right. Meanwhile they stride from mountain to mountain, all those who did not fit into the car anymore. Breath fumes at them from fathomless chasms. We are Titans, they say, they keep telling us, but they don't say: Whose breath could this be? Is it the Titans' or does it belong to a small party of small people, conservative to the core, with careers solid and lusterless drab? And this is also us, such a small domain had we secured for ourselves. We are the little guys, the ones who are breathing, we must do that, except: We are not *we*. We are *me*, only *me*, that does something to me, we being me! For once, just for a trial, I am all there is, all and everyone, that doesn't mean I am none at all, done in by all. I am speaking here, I am the only one talking, period. Greetings to you, my home, yes and also to you my hearth. You must once again experience the *Kehre*, the *Turn*, time for a thorough cleansing, uhm, cleaning, but not today. And those people here, all people, welcome! Come on in, I have plenty of room! My house is not surrounded by men. Thank God! And the father not in tears, the father is long dead. I am joining in now to find out on TV the lot that befell other houses but not mine. There are still others, I could whisper in your ear, but on principle I never whisper. I stay put and shut up.

Little drives us more than the thought that the Greeks incur debts, even though they really shouldn't. And now the engine's broken down, I am sorry, but it will have to be repaired first, or we won't be driven by anything anymore and if anything still drives us it is the worry about this country, for those fanatics shall not tell us what to do without impunity, never again. They've never done it? But they would love to. OK and now we'll drive with our families to our own church, which has been reformed long ago, albeit not for everyone. We're driving to our reformed church, which would never summon us to our Lord. We come voluntarily. And our breath is like the smoke of a sacrifice, but those who are getting killed are non-smokers, well, maybe not, but they can't smoke anymore with their heads sawed off, cut off, their bodies light clouds our God tramples down like morning dew raised by the sun, for the sun also rises every day, that's pretty clear and the day is also clearing up. Is that clear? No. It is hard for us to assert ourselves in our party system. So we just assert something else.

He, however, yes, he, he continues to dwell at feasts everlasting around his gold tables? You don't say! And there are still more of you? All homemade? He the One? And taking pleasure only in us? So I can come, just me, all by myself, so I can come, oh dear, I beat you in virtue great God, I can do that, I'll show you, you tell me, I'll show you. Look here, let's take one as an example. Let's take Zeus, that won't offend anyone, not even our reformer, not our movement and not our rigidness, for no one believes in that one. I had to think quite a while until I thought of him. I don't dare to pick another one or the Greeks will beat me up, who of course are entitled to their own Gods, so then, let's take Zeus, whom I have beaten—he's no longer competition—whom I have beaten in virtue. Whatever else he can do, you can hear in Richard Wagner, but there he's got another name, anyone can have his own opinion about that as far as I'm concerned. But futzing around with women, that's a no-no. Into the women's favor you stole yourself, Zeus, that's an absolute no-no, I wouldn't do such a thing, because my God says no, he prohibits what you have done, could my God have done that too? Probably, or he wouldn't have existed for as long as you have not existed, Zeus, or what or whoever, uncalled you came to the Greeks' camp, you fucked the women relentlessly, by the dozen you fucked them, that was enough for you, but rescuing your people was not your thing. That God. That just wasn't his thing. And he could have done it so easily. Maybe he didn't know they were in trouble? This couldn't happen to our God, he knows everything, the other one just claims he does, but ours knows everything, he even knows when someone sketches something, when he draws his best friend, the prophet, he knows what that drawing is supposed to represent, even if somewhat distorted, or it would be a photo, wouldn't it, and would be owned by Germany, who owns everything. This God, I have to look up which one, he is one by whom another one claims he's been insulted, it was an act of sacrilege, so now we must kill everyone, everyone?, never! Not even with the greatest effort will your hand accomplish this, it'll break off sooner; that God sees the small drawing, since he can see everything, and he says, fine with me, but I don't know what my prophet will have to say to it, I do have my worries there, still, enraged as you are, no sorrow shall befall you, no harm done to you, for I couldn't care less, also about all the drama you are creating and about the uproar, which will crumble because of bad advice, as good advice comes at a price, which you can't afford, on how to save this foreigner-flooded country, none of those guys knows how to do that, but I do! They know how to kill someone, but not how to save him, he doesn't know that, that blind-minded, dim-witted and not at all just God, as my several million assistants, a-socials, asses, are promoting me as if I were a cash cow, what do you make of me?, how much off me?, no idea why I am always getting such bad press, that's not OK with me, they say I am a God who always wreaks vengeance, but never rights wrongs. How often have I written this already?, doesn't matter, it'll soon be over. Then it's your turn and that's all she wrote. You savage centaurs, who have four healthy limbs each but use only two for the trigger, so what are you doing with your two feet which carried you to where you have no business? You stand on them looking pretty stupid, just like you present me and simply gun down those who portray me, who portray my prophet. Yes, don't look at me so baffled! It's you, only you! I come with my virile strength, no one dares to open his mouth and I say: It's you. Guarded by wide sections of the population who is riddled with rot it blows one's top. That's why we say: Something's brewing among the population. You are it, you'll soon be foaming over yourselves!

But human flesh is just too tempting, isn't it?! Tastes good, the gruesome meal that belongs to HIM, but we can have one taste of the flesh, there's no soul in it anymore, which could make the flesh taste bitter, death threatens: youyouyou! So now get the soul out with the spear and one two three into the oven with it! Shame stays far from that Goddess of violence, we never visit her. Luckily she lives so far away. She always lives farther than us. But somehow we'll manage to get there. Exactly. When the car comes back from its service, we'll make a drive, we'll drive there. She rages some other place. That's where we want to go, to the house of Atlas?, no, we'll never make it that far up to the top! So we won't go. Not everyone will approve, nonetheless we won't go there. We have another excuse, it makes no difference either, for besides us no one's talking anyway. Violence runs riot elsewhere. And afterwards, when nothing's left alive, not even violence, everyone says: It is done, yes, but what? They didn't accomplish much with their stupid violence that drags anyone no longer able to walk out of his bed, and no one will get up anymore, not even a statue. That's what they did, those shadows with their stupid flags, which they hold up to the beaming light to get a good photo and video. They are completely absorbed in their work, and for starters this or that statue will be overturned. OK, all of them will fall. Whatever we can't sell, we'll overturn, they say, you know, who. I rather not say it out loud, or I'll fall too, and only yesterday I sprained my arm during the balance exercise, for which I wouldn't even have needed my arm. I get down to work and write. They get down to their work and destroy texts, the written words, it goes much faster to make those disappear. And I, and I, and I will disappear even faster, wanna bet? There they are already severing a head from the torso again, with inadequate tools, you can actually see how hard they have to work to get that head off. Feeding it all to the dogs? Maybe later, first we have to film everything, so that everyone knows about it. All the ungrateful inhabitants of this city who don't want to obey we'll slay them all with our glowing weapons, they are so happy, look how they gleam, those weapons. We filmed it all, look! Isn't it great, how we bring them all down with our fast bullets! And those who can still get bullets are quite lucky. The city fills up with the dead and the rivers get their waters freshly dyed. Who is next to lend my support to? If my writing won't save you, it's been wasted. Today you are not yet ready to die? It doesn't matter, we'll take care of it, I daresay and I say it: God is great. But I can't really see him very well, maybe he isn't such a biggie? But if you say so it's probably right. Who should I look at and where is my measuring tape anyway, I still had it yesterday, for the new sofa. How come he must be big? How in God's name could you ever have done what you did? It's not possible without knowing exactly how big this God is, just a moment, I'll be right there, I found the tape and I'll measure him. It's said so often how big he is, so that many really believe it, I'd like to know for sure. They kill everybody, but they are supposed to spare the children? No, they don't spare the children, why just the children? Exactly. Listen: So somebody says: I'll kill your children. My mother answers him: Do whatever you want! It is your right. Do, as you like it! But kill me first! The man said: That's not worth it. You'll die of grief anyway. And he cut off the legs of my two children. Yes, their legs were cut off indeed. My mother pleaded one more time with her neighbor who did it to kill her. Now a girl appears (she'll disappear again later) and says: Wait, you will soil your clothes. Take them off! And as mom doesn't obey fast enough, the girl throws her on her back and tears her clothes off her body. At that moment another man comes by. He carries a lance and with all his strength he pushes it in my mother's back. And then they left. What? What happened next? A lot happens next, but I stop here, no one's listening anyway. Forget it! You can omit it and forget it. Cut it, otherwise I'll have to do it myself! And what could you do anyway? Nothing. For a change.

If they had spared anyone, how could they be called the radiant ones. OK. The work is done, the killing, a service only to HIM, shamelessly they abuse everyone, big guys and small folks, you know whom I mean. By force they drag them from their beds, exactly, we can relate to that, we do that too, like the scum on filthy dishwater they stand at our threshold, they won't get any beds from us. Let them go elsewhere. Let them get on the busses and go some place else where there are fewer people and they would be needed.

But it's always someone else who's supposed to do it, right, we are prospective avengers, but not in person, we would like to be, but at the decisive moment we chicken out and issue a press release or we make a drawing or we just talk into a void pierced by two hundred microphones. Those are pretty small before God, they are even too small for us! Nevertheless, they offer many tongues, which don't have to be cut out, they must be heard, after all. We're just talking. Let someone else do it. I am mocking Him, unfortunately I can't draw, OK, so I try, but nothing comes of it, I mock in writing, that much I can do, it's not always easy either, let me tell you. Oral doesn't work at all for me, speech, the jewel that adorns the dead, but only once, at the funeral, I am not clad in speech for armour. I reach for it, oh God, but it is gone! Yesterday it was still where I put it, but today there's only a telephone, which has its own language and doesn't need me to speak. It's been misplaced again, the stupid language. The telephone can't replace it, it does know my words, but not all of them, no way!, I don't even use them all myself. I am afraid of them. And I didn't eat it. It's inedible. No, it isn't with the editor, he says it is ineditible, that idiot language, it'll never find its way back home to me. And the editor says he doesn't have it and he couldn't edit it anyway. I must have left it somewhere, it is no longer at my command. Oh my God, help! oh no, then he might show up too! I lock his door, I mean the door of that God, I've no idea whose turn it is this time, the smartphone didn't ring, but he doesn't want to come in person, that God, he is like a waterfall, no, I better not turn him into some Niagara fall, I shut him in and I shut myself off from him , so he can't get out anymore, at least so he won't get to me, even though he can do everything, accomplish everything, he won't get in here and he isn't on the phone either, he can't just be called that easily, if you had hoped to do so.

The killing will take place over there today. If you made it all the way to here you'll be able to find the place. It's located in any other portable phone as well. Everyone can hear it, it can call anyone if it wants to, it lives in any computer, in anyone who can neither read nor write but is able to operate a device, well, I am not, unfortunately, I can write occasionally, but not talk, think, feel, anything really, I come to my own country cautiously and in secret so that I won't notice when I'm there. Was that another call just now, I heard a little melody coming from there, which I don't know, so that wasn't my language? Where was it, whose was it? I was just told that 80 million Turks are practically allowed to settle anywhere—except here, as long as we exist in our present mode we insist: not here! But that wasn't told to me, only to another telephone, which rang differently than mine. OK. Maybe I don't have a telephone, well, I do have one but I never use it. No one can reach me? Whom do you wish to speak? I doesn't exist, maybe you want to proceed on safe ground and speak to someone else? Let me tell you—other children also have beautiful devices. No need to call me. I don't know me and I have no idea, I never learned how to operate this device, I am not a surgeon, I don't even cut into my own texts. And whoever can operate this text doesn't have to know how writing functions, he only has to get the picture, no, take one, make one, just a small picture whereof the saying goes thou shalt not do that; I should not make myself an image of someone I know as little as my telephone, we should look at—yes, why not also at the display of the telephone, where the head is shown, though not where it belongs but where it was resolutely taken in hand. The body lies next to it. Resentment and anger were expressed here undisguised, not fury, fury would have passed too quickly, anger, however, acts correctly, even though not politically correct. I'd like to do that too, take my head in hand resolutely, it seems to be quite easy, even if it is quite an effort to go through with it, they don't use a sword, he who takes up a sword, shall die by the sword, that's why they use a kind of kitchen knife, don't they?, they are allowed to do that, armed with that they may even sit at the table of their fathers and their heavenly father, he wouldn't feel threatened by such a knife, and yet this very head gets cut off now by the culture heroes—who nevertheless hate culture, and that means every culture— and placed before God, please accept this small sacrifice, sure, go ahead, but where is the body that goes with it, what should I do just with the head?, no head transplant has ever been successful. Luckily he doesn't ask me this question, I do not belong to his body that is embedded in the center of the sky's vaulted throne and now that body reaches for another head to see whether it fits him better than his own. No. He can't have mine either, no need to look at me so demandingly, that God, mine is still attached, or isn't this my head? Head first I fall into the dust of my home, the new rulers of Greece have also just arrived, well, that's all we needed!, but don't we want to welcome them?, no, we hate their blaspheming heads and throw them to the dogs, for they do not want to pay their debts. Though we are the ones to blame as they claim! We are to blame for their blunders, says he whom we did nothing but good! But their Gods who took off long ago—only the Greeks haven't noticed yet and think, they'll help them—so their Gods say something else, nothing can be done about it, against our bulwarks they shall crash, in their ships they shall drown, with our quick-wingèd arrows they shall be killed if they won't pay, they will see what they get out of it, well, now, they've already got a lot of it, since we don't get it. They keep it. Their Gods want them to keep what they have, OK, it's only one God, actually, only one, one piece of Godhead. I, unfortunately, could not even keep in mind what I wanted to say now. How can I talk to you about keeping anything?! I am filled with the blood of the dead, I've had enough, it drives me out of my mind, that people are constantly dying who wouldn't yet have to, who haven't yet practiced it. And that takes time. We should be their rescuers, and what are we? Their murderers. And our waves turn blood red. It poses no risk, not even a residual risk for me saying this here. I can say everything, and I am allowed to do so. It doesn't even have to happen in a certain order, which I've broken long ago. It makes no sense, says this gentleman, he is talking about Turkey joining the EU, it goes against the grain, it doesn't add up, messing up the proper sequence that way! There are others already in line! Let go of my arm, will you! You are already in arms way! OK, what I've got here now, well, not really me personally, but anyway, a very small amount has been set for future payments which cannot be undercut any further, because the Greeks have absolutely no more money, and less than nothing doesn't work. More always does.

It's so cheap, me saying all this. It costs me nothing. I waste it on you, I throw it up in the air like paper scraps, like money, which, after all, is nothing else. Listen, it's different everywhere else, but not here. Here it is like it is here! To rob others of their fortunes, the Greeks no longer want to pay us anything, oh Gods, just tell them they should pay, what else is left for them to do? Nothing's left for them! Because!, what they don't pay, they rob from us! For their fortune back home has been squandered by luxuries and scattered by idleness. Let them croak, and here they go. A few more just hit the bucket. They are dying all the time, jumping out of windows, from cliffs, from chairs, out of trains, they don't want it any other way. They don't want to pay, that's monstrous, and their God is a monster, oh no!, I am afraid I am talking about something entirely different now, I just don't know it yet. It's all the same anyway. Maybe about their neighbors? Could very well be, because they look pretty much alike, one can hardly distinguish them, that's just like them!, but the neighbors returned home later, late returnees from sunless grounds' dark night, but we cannot respect their grounds, they come from another God, we do not want to mess with. He is not the guardian of the house, he only guards the Turks and a few more billions elsewhere which we don't miss here, unlike the Greeks who do very much. Instead of being careful not to enrage us—the swarm of their foes—being led to their demise against their hope of not having to pay, that's what's going to happen, I am afraid.

I mock this God, yes, I mock satanically, so does my colleague over there, I screech, I scream like a saw milling through tiles, an especially nasty noise, cutting heads off is somewhat more muted, luckily, witnesses report it sounds like a car running over a cat. That doesn't mean anything to me. Those people will stop screaming soon, because they don't have anymore air to breathe, the head falls off, so it is tossed some place, no, it is put on an uninhabited torso, after it's been photographed for the album, no, not for the family album, that one does not belong to the family, anyway, it gets photographed and filmed and kept in memory by one or another. Maybe the picture can still be useful later. I mock, I mock and I finish nothing. For 'It is finished' already belongs to a God, one moment, please, I have to check this, no, I don't have that one in stock either. Anyway, mocking is easy. But killing the mockers is a lot of work, well, not that much either, you can get to the murder scene by car and the killing is done by the weapon, the automatic weapon, every child can do it. Not mocking, that's more difficult, but doing away with people, killing people, that's a cinch. Maybe that's why it's so popular? Could be. I also rather do things that aren't work.

I take over, I just don't know what from whom. I wander about like one of the centaurs, are those mountain climbers? Snow enthusiasts? What does Auschwitz tell them? It tells them an awful lot, one can't drill it often enough into the their fellow citizens tender personalities. It goes right through them. The Centaurs? That's those people in weird get-ups, their destiny piled up high on their shoulders, that only sports can win them security?, no idea, but those people will be hit with bloody bows and swept away, erased, we won't get all of them, but as many as possible, in the mountains, by whatever means, blot them out, send them death with winged projectiles, the blowout should also be a gas, press a key, delete, all gone!, yes, it all comes out right here in front, but nothing comes of it, and people also become fewer and fewer; they follow their God, they greet their God, God bless and then they go on without him and then they go under. They get buried under an avalanche or they choose themselves where and how. They greet their hearth, everyone's got one of those, even the poorest, they look their dwelling in its kind eyes, yes, here they were at home, and then they were gone. Kidnapping, murder, slaughter no longer necessary. Cancer still necessary, but not always and everywhere.

OK. Here is the sacred shrine, let's go inside. The pope is already looking forward to seeing you. Africa says, that's our Lourdes, that's where we like to pray. We already watched the Holy Mary's appearances and Mary even has her own radio. Her son may use it too. In this church, people will be safe, this is Africa, after all, and not the wilderness, not just a dark continent. And this is God, here, may I introduce— his mother over there, she makes an appearance every so often, this is a peaceful place, or she certainly would never come. The pope says so too. Peace be with you, but not with your spirit, that one can fume and rage and burst like flames out of the bodies rather than into them, like at Pentecost. Everything that happens is God's wish and his mother also says: Yes, I want it too, whatever my son wants, who became my boss while he was growing up, yes, I also want it then, come!, this is my darling son, in whom I am well pleased, or did his father say that? No, I think it was a disembodied voice, so it probably was the radio. I can't remember right now, but here is the church, you are there, come on in all of you! We speak this into the radio and out of it, in Africa we have a lot of sex, or do I mean sexes, might I mean sorts, could we agree on sorts?, OK, here we have only two, but that means one too many. It has to go. They all believe in God, but one sort believes in the right one. Well, yes, both of you may come, albeit not all the time, this time one sort is coming, the other one must go, next time it may be the other way around. Who doesn't believe this? Well, I do. Who doesn't believe, because he is an infidel and not over-whelmed by the spirit of God? Every bad seed—and that means always the other one, the one which one is not must retreat and make room. It must be exterminated if it does not want to retreat. We provide the terminator. One group moves in, others move out, that is Africa, a constant coming and going, like everywhere else. People say: We are coming in now. That means the others can't get out of the church

anymore, which was built by master builders of the civiliza-
tion of love. The eyes of the clergy light up. The radio for-
bids the infidels to live. No, they can't get in here, those
people, there is no room for them, not in this church, and if
they do get in, it is only to get killed, as interestingly as possible, in a way that might never have been done before, but
it probably has, people are so inventive. Just a moment, I
wanted to say, they don't get out anymore, not out of Africa,
not out of the world, not even out of this church. So the
hunt starts, happy trails in the land of God, nowhere are
folks more Catholic than here, unfortunately not all of
them, not altogether all of them, whoever is not is the first
one dead. Thus, life is pleasant and carefree in view of the
beyond, which gets painted in especially nice and friendly
colors for their religion, the paint's already running down
the walls. That's being promised; salvation is constantly
announced, not just by the radio of Jesus and the Virgin
Mary. It gets promoted everywhere and that's it. Whoever
hasn't heard it is dead. They are going, they have to go, no,
not all of them, they are driven to where the toilets were.
So let the young man finally speak, he's been waiting forever,
even though he isn't the Eternal One, let's not interrupt him!
We have been ordered to get on board as he commences to
speak. But too many people are in there already. So this other
man, a neighbor, starts laughing and says: Oh no, this is
Africa, even if just a small section of it, but an important
one, it is occupied, the toilet, let's go to a ditch where the
corpses get thrown in, and he pushed us in. It was a kind of
toilet, a latrine, it got into our mouths, the ears, everywhere.
Then he tossed a few stones on top of us and moved a thick
cinder plate across the hole. I tried to climb out, but it was

sealed very well. Inside, it was completely dark. This is Africa, even if not the whole of it. But if we travel too much in foreign lands, we'll lose the rest of our minds. Our lives lie in your hands, Mr Bishop, Sir, Mr Priest, Mr Such and Such, we request a conversation with you, so you can pass this on to God, but we don't get it. This is not a conversation, these are horrible screams coming from the outside into the church. Even the dignitary can't ignore them, the screams drown out even the voice of God, it doesn't matter, it also comes out of the radio and that can be turned louder, whatever you want. Or you don't have to listen at all so you can say later, you haven't heard a thing. There's a dog running along with a hand in his snout. It could have been mine, however, not my dog, for I don't have one. I am not referring to myself. God's deputy is talking here, he also talks on the radio, his voice resounds, and he says: Kill anyone who isn't you! That's a pretty simple message. People are listening, and then they don't get out anymore, because it is too late. The action in the slaughterhouse has begun. Voices are raised and they are screaming and screaming, otherwise no one rises anymore.

Though, actually, they are getting out when they think they are getting in. They can't make out where the inside is and the outside, they got home too late, they took the wrong turn. As blessed spirits they took the wrong turn up the free-way ramp, no, they turned to Europe, wrong track, they are on the wrong track, not on mine anyway, they are not on my track, that's good, well said, all right then, I am going in, but as always it is an out. The people are gone. They are going in the wrong direction and already they are done in.

They are Nazis now and have no God. They rage, nobody stops them, what for, it's good for them. Their bodies expanded. Some bodies are heavy, but not all bodies in general. Those are. Well, they weigh heavily on me, because I can't grasp them properly to be able to lift them. Let's drop it now, we do not judge. But judgements are certainly not incidental, it's just that I can't grasp the healthy difference between the ones and the others. This reading in this bookstore must not take place here, I say, I judge, because the problem already starts with a reading. What problem? No idea, but I do know: Whoever isn't with us is against us. You know it, because you've been told. You call upon a figure of the past to live again. You don't like something and you also say so. What is it you don't like, would you like to move backward in spirit until you get to an un-time, to an un-Godly spirit who did not expect you and has not yet cleaned up? No, they reply, that's not what we want. We want to announce a new time in which the mind will no longer have anything to say. This will be their time and it will have tremendous dimensions. They are not Nazis now and they have a God, for whom they let themselves be killed and would also kill themselves, those are a different breed and they have a new party, there's no better one far and wide. An alternative, which is already an alternative, all of them are for Germany, which is alive, it could also have been totally destroyed. So, his most loyal followers are raging in front of this bookstore, where the reading is taking place today. Someone's talking who is not for us and therefore against us; and while the reader reads and the listeners listen, the crowd at the gates turns back home, but it's an Out not an In, this home, as they turn themselves in to the sunless grounds of the night, which has no grounds to look so darkly, the ground can be found in nature. Everyone loves having his grounds in nature, that way one knows one's plots and can overlook them. Today for once the night does not take place, it seems to want to stay light. Lots of torching here tonight. Still, time says it's night. Time is not corruptible, or the city would be up in arms and unrestrained. Events planned for the night would take place in bright daylight. Many see a fight as a sort of consecration. I see nothing, I am sitting too far in the back, could you please keep your head more to the left, so I can look forward to the right. So the reading against the new party, one barely listened do, for who'd be able to write then?, the reading is still going on, however, I am not writing this in real time, the times are real enough for me. There is screaming outside, a humming as of insects, a din, a circle of maybe 20 people, their torches sticking out of their bodies, some holding up self-made signs, guide posts to the new time. It is followed by a heavy ballad which, nonetheless, will soon be blowing in the wind, which won't let itself be stopped by the time. But they also could be killed, that happens very quickly, without any warning. That doesn't guarantee instant success, but what has this German *Volk* not endured already! No wonder, a grand huge building has been dedicated to it!, they deserved it, since the building had been destroyed. Insert the name that's close to you, but I don't know where. No one sings, no one says anything, they are getting the daylight scared out of them without the cover of night.

Someone's finally pushing in the door code to end something; two persons enter and kill twelve, who, allegedly, but

who knows?, have no God and don't acknowledge the murderers' God nor anyone else's. They get decimated, that's
how it's called. That's now the word for it. They are Nazis,
they are not Nazis and now they are partying. They are
having a ball and are going to dance. No, a God has prohibited it. But they can drive a car, out of their neighborhood,
where the prices are right, oh Father, is it also right for the
children to protect their father? Well, actually, he should do
it for them, but the sons hate the Father's enemies and hurry,
though not all too quickly, oh yes, yes, they are quickly on
their way, up the stairs, pulling the trigger and doing the
deed, which one can always do if one lacks worldly goods.

We are still contemplating, we are contemplating something
else, whether we are Nazis or would rather have another
identity that is independent of everything that exists. I'd also
like such a one. Why are we not National Socialists? Well,
we are somehow, today that's possible again; it's perfectly
OK to go by what has been! Or not? Our parents and grand-
parents were much wronged! They were heroes, not crimi-
nals! Are we deploring the spirit of destruction in these dark
times? All right, fine. In the old days we could call for the
time, it was announced on the dot, done, now we can no
longer call it off, because it gets shown to us everywhere, on
every device in our hands. We cannot call off night's shadows, when they get traded, as always, against shining light.
We are citizens, we worked through the nights and visited
state assemblies, which immediately dissembled, the mem-
bers had a fall-out, it didn't help that we went there. We'll
have a vote, every voice counts, says one secretary general,
who, however, did not get elected. All of this is very small,

but wants to grow. We are looking for natural allies. Naturally we are looking for allies, at night they are already standing outside and brutally wreck this reading in a bookstore, where an author wants to get down to his work; no, they don't do that, they can't make it work, they are only around twenty people with stupid names which should all be changed, albeit not in our name. We can refer to precedents, to what had counted in another time, OK, let's do that. We can be others! Yes, that's what we'll do right now! We are different as of now. We miss something somehow, something that has been, but we are others now and don't need it anymore. As the ones who we were, we still needed it. We no longer do. We still needed the knowledge, some sense as mentioned before, of something missing, the University is a mess, though it is missed. Ignorance ignites, knowledge is burnt out, it is sorely missed, but not by me. It means nothing to me anymore, it has no more value to me, it no longer counts, the university is broke, no, it broke down, thus it destroyed all knowledge and strangled all desire for knowledge. We no longer need clever impartation, we don't mourn its loss. We turn it on and we turn it off. When the screen is on, we find out in the smallest and most unpleasant way, for the screen is small, isn't it, everything must fit on it for a bit, you too, little baby Jesus, here you can look out of the screen without shielding us, without sheltering us as others their father, that's their strength; no kidding!, what's next?, doesn't matter, our unavoidable massive essence will look into it and then again out of it even before we can be shown the dulling accounting of successes, yes. That's our God. But we couldn't care less about him, though this doesn't mean he matters to no one, he does, but as another one. Another God does matter to others. We get personal too, yes, we can do that too, we are not aiming for closeness to life—who is still close to us anyway? What will be important, attention now, I won't say it twice, is securing the original certainty in choosing and deciding, not with regard to a partner for life, but in terms of our has-been-ness. Not just because we cannot retain anything and everything and that's just in terms of capacity. So someone has deserted, forsaken us, and now he forces me to deal with that has-been-ness once again and include it in the what-has-to-be, which I did not have in mind originally. I wanted to forget it. But the experience of being deserted continues to shape the given and this awakens it in all its anticipation of dominating power. But what do I do with power, if I can't exercise it now! That's what makes me so angry! I can't bear it! I can't bear having been forsaken and this makes me seethe with anger.

Therefore, I want to tell you: It already happened by way of the unconscious—which is looking for reality, not the other way around, no way the other way around!—that I have now experienced the double life of Hans in reality. He leaves the restaurant with me, his purported motive: hunger, that's what drives him away from me, and in the next restaurant he meets his new object of desire, which he had already found after he was done with me, no, actually, even before he was done with me, and curses me with the following sentence: It just doesn't work! Well. I also went to the restaurant, I followed him of course, I was upset and went immediately to the toilet and—both gone, when I got back from the toilet, then outside his pointed remark: It just doesn't work! What doesn't work, he, just leaving the restaurant, just so, at 9 p.m. to meet—at the same restaurant where we had met as a couple for 15 years—his new lover, who, conveniently enough, also lives in the 9th district, with her partner, the attorney? Why did both leave? Why don't they stand by their love or desire in my presence? What confrontation gets avoided here? They have their desire, I have mine, which doesn't do me any good, since the only thing left is this connection to our has-been-ness and I've got my loneliness, this double-play is an annihilation. We all are split, but would you, for example, you, the way I know you, choose this kind of split? You create unambiguity for your character, maybe this is petrification, no idea, you, in any case can't deal with exchangeability. I long for escaping the circle of the constant lie, my intuition feels it and I don't want to give in to it and yet: My intuition is right—the moment Hans leaves, he's going to the other one without an interval, it's pure desire. Only, what prevents the two of them to live this desire without the other two (me and her lover, the attorney)? My attitude towards Hans was: I have been wronged, that is, his desire for another entered my life as reality, that is why he has to carry out the separation from me, because I never felt the wish to separate. He has to leave, I won't manage the separation for him, it would not be my own desire. And yet, by his staging of the exchange Hans accomplished my leaving, because otherwise I would have lost part of my self-respect. That shock: He walks out of the restaurant where we sit, just for a moment, he says, he'll be right back, I call him, several times and he's sitting with Lisi in our favourite place. OK. I come and both of them leave. I choke. I really think I'll choke to death. Like every new movement, every

new partnership, whatever, everything new runs into danger
that with all this emphasis on the new and different it will
cut itself off from the great tradition and get lost in awk-
wardness and half-truths. That is why he must split up with
me. He must. Not I. I insist on it. I won't split up with him.
He must do it. He has to carry it out. He has to carry out
the separation. I don't want it after all. I don't want to. He
has to. I can't. He must do it.

When we still had some knowledge, we seemed quite bright
and still we brought nothing to light. We easily get over what
has happened and what should be and isn't. No, we don't
need a God, believe me, and if I say it a thousand times,
maybe you'll believe me. It really would be better that way,
but you believe in something else anyway, at least you
believe—thus showing some balance—how space and time
shed light on each other, until they become invisible, because
we are dead. But this is a dependency I would not wish for.
I don't want to be dependent on time, space I could at least
make for myself. But we, we don't need him, God, and they
don't need him either, whoever they are. But they say they
need their God. And whoever doesn't need him—Wham!-
Bam-Pow—gets whacked, offed with automatics, whose
principle is: If one pulls the trigger, it releases the hammer,
I think I already explained the rest, the effect is robust—oh
no, not you, my God!, I mean the other one, you there—in
so many ways, and it always works, always and anywhere,
you can always kill someone anywhere in your expansive,
fruitless territories, yes, I like the fruitless ones, I'll buy that
one, with pleasure, always and anywhere, even where the
trees' arms resist me, where a no-stopping sign resists me,

where a locked cold-storage room prevents me, where a wrongly inserted number on an entrance door could have prevented it, it couldn't, we've got the right number, we enter now, and then we eliminate another number, a number of people, a few little cartoonists, no more than that, and there won't be more, this is how they get punished, nice people, it's no fun, my friends envy me this job, they'd have liked to shoot too, but they are abroad, where they also shoot, but at others, not unknown on earth or among Gods, that is, at Mr President, those men to whose house we were sent, there are no pathless deserts to soothe, no wild sea to calm down, we simply get inside with the door code and done, our trespasser hands already take action, and done, done, done! Sustained fire!

Our grandfathers were no heroes, we didn't know them, but we are. We don't understand their deeds and only make the absent accountable. The killing is over, but as for dying, anyone can do that, we sign whatever is put in front of us, the cartoonists won't be able to do much more, rather less, well, let me tell you—even though they are famous: They are not much more than we, the little guys, so they can draw, but the wrong thing, that's all there is to them, defiling the prophet, we can do that without drawings. When the prophet does come some day, we won't defile him, that's the difference, but even that he could take the wrong way, next to his wrath lightning would be a breath of pain, killed by his own people, a murder millions would see on TV and they'd just have to press the remote control. That hasn't worked before, we won't do it to our God this time, luckily he never appears to us, the prophet, let alone the God, we only call him, but if he came for real one day, he'd only be mocked, and we would be justified to do it, it's best we don't do anything at all. But he doesn't appear, I think he didn't appear to those who believed in him either, therefore we don't know what he looks like; those cartoonists, however, they do know and they use this knowledge, they don't simply defend the customary, they give the prophet a new look, which we, however, don't know either and can't compare, we don't know the original, we only know the old view that he exists, we've never seen the prophet, but others did and they say he doesn't look like in these drawings, we lay our hands into the fire for this and even like to eat them as soon as they are done, we eat our own hands, when they have sinned and we sit on our ears, as the saying goes, so that we hear nothing and we sever the shameless heads from the torsos and throw them to the dogs. And the city's ungrateful inhabitants are slaughtered by this shining weapon, a simple kitchen knife with which they can't cut even the mustard anymore, or they are taken out by our fast projectile, no, many projectiles, this house has also got some, and we are coming, we are coming, and the river will turn red with blood. Really? Do you really think that now the prophet does look like in this drawing? No human being looks like that, seeing this, even the ocean's waves roar with laughter, he must have looked different in earlier days, for they don't recognize him, even though he once walked across those waves, no, that was the other one—the competition, doesn't matter, we kill them all anyway, but we know as little about what he looks like, and we don't have to know, he's not our business, we kill those who believe in this one and that one, period. But nobody looks like these drawings and no God

either and no prophet who throws himself tearfully at his
God's chest because he is much more beautiful, people are
so mean the way they represent him! They don't know at all
what I look like, yet they draw pictures of me, they see me
wrongly, they don't see me as a benefactor but as ridiculous,
they ridicule me, says the prophet; who could still believe in
my Lord with such a misshapen person vouching for him?,
well, that doesn't work, that won't do, I should send them a
newer image of myself, then they wouldn't have to do it,
you shall not make for yourself an image, the Gorgons knew
that already, hissing loudly, eyes flashing skywards out of
glistering heads, but no one shows up there, as usual. We
are here now, looking into their red glowing eyes—that's
because of the flash—everything looking somewhat unnat-
ural, a beginner's mistake, they would have had to turn off
the automatic, what did I want to say?, hah!, a God quickly
dives down to us lucky ones and gives us the photo of his
prophet: this is exactly what he looks like, just like that, this
really is the original, you want to claim we photographed
someone else? You aren't saying that?, good. Just like that.
Remember that!, and woe to you if you show him differently, he will lament, he will pursue you, and then a lot more
people will have reason to pursue you, we'll sue you, it is a
distorted, disfiguring depiction like any old picture, it just
shows something, it's not telling; and I, who am I anyway?,
a God plus prophet, not the one who wanted to kill his son,
please!, that's another God, but the son wanted it that way,
he wanted it his way or no way, that idiot, and now? Stunned
by horror, he flees this way and that, hides in his poor
mother's gown, in the column's shade, ducks at the altar
hearth—even before the last supper he doesn't dare to go

out—ducks down there, duckling-like. The mother screams, someone's screaming, is it the mother?, it is a woman's voice and it screams: What are you doing, father? This cannot be, this is no place for women, not even when they lament the murder of their child, their only son, the father wanted it that way, the son complied, isn't that nice, such unity in the trinity?, they all scream, the father screams, the servants scream, the son screams, the mother screams, but the father drives the son around the column, the food's already on the table, but the father chases the son around in a circle, the food gets cold, now look at that, he confronts the father with the sharp knife, or was it the man he sent off with the knife to kill his own son? It wasn't meant seriously though, it was just a dress rehearsal! The performance could not take place, because someone stole the rock upon which the sacrifice should have been offered up, better, if he'd stolen the knife it would have been less of an effort, no, no, it was him, it was God himself, he has the violence monopoly and he demands a high price for it, personally he would like it to be different, but that doesn't work, he pierces the son's liver, no, not yet, the son isn't dead yet, he is going to die like everyone else, as everyone has to die, falling backwards and breathing his last breath or falling flat on his face, forward-facing, that also works, and that father, can you believe it!, shouts for joy, because there's yet another one getting into heaven, where there'll be more joy over him than over ninety-nine righteous people, who always list the exact amount of their income and always get humiliated by braggarts, who designed the successful detour of money while others crashed with their SUVs into the construction site. Making a God disappear is simple, money is quite a bit more difficult. No, for now it's just the son, yes, he, he's the one.

The father, his murderer, his father wanted it that way, didn't he, his father, the murderer, not the father's murderer, the father as the killer of the son, despite the son's compliance, a murder no less, and he calls out with relief: I toppled my son with my own hand, and he atoned for the sin of the father, who should be closest to stand by the son, he atoned for his father's hatred with his own blood. OmyGod, nothing to be done about that, as for me, I protect my prophet. No one protected the prophet over there. To be on the safe side, we also point the knife at others, who are trying to hide, at an altar, is that an altar? I can't really see it, some sort of excrescence, some excretion of the earth, especially made for a God and that's where he's hiding, the son of God, that's where he comes out of now, the son, his hands reaching up pleadingly towards chin and neck, and what does he scream? If your deeds don't save but, rather, destroy us, they are wasted missed deeds indeed, no, that's not what he calls out: Oh dearest father, do not kill me! You already finished off the other one, please, do not have me killed! That's a lot of gobbledigod! The God I know has only one son, whom he let be killed and watched it too, but that's understandable, I can understand this like any murder among relatives and married couples or generally people who know each other well. Late, but better than never everyone gets to the point of retribution. The method of payment is death, there is no credit card for it. The killing won't get postponed, except circumstances require otherwise. Death is the payment, the killer cannot be restrained. How could we still have hope?

We can't. I am yours, says the son, says every son in every language, but that's not the case. Who is this, please? One who madly rolls his eyes, fuming with fury, that's some gaze, Gorgon-like, I've never seen such a gaze, and then he raises his club, as blacksmiths do when they hit the hoof. The women, who lock the monstrous in the shape of horses— they won't settle for anything smaller inside themselves— want it that way, riding is their life, that's the secret of women. One must strike when the iron is hot, one must kill as long as one is filled with fury—often it doesn't last very long—and raise the gun and lower it again, over the boy's head, lower the wood down to the boy's blond forehead and break his skull. Thus died the second son, the talk is always about the first one, we didn't even know there were more sons, so now we also hear about brothers, the order has been given and taken, the weapon has been delivered and now he delivers!— you'd better believe it! He has already killed one of the brothers and is on his way to the third victim, whom, how- ever, the God cannot find. I think two are already one too many, there is only one as spread by tradition and sprung from the book, not mine, *the* Book. But now, please really lock the door! If I were God, I wouldn't kill my son, but I don't have one; who knows what I would be capable of if I had one; here is a photo—no, not of my son, I don't have one—of my prophet, thank God, and that's the truth, now we know what he got to look like in the meantime, old, he got old, didn't he, the beard makes him look even older, it already did when he was young, now we all know it, we know him, we would recognize him in the street, we have the latest picture, the one by those cartoonists was a full- blown effrontery, which made us furious, our youthful heads, our women in bikinis, at least one of them who as of late no longer wanted to allow anymore research, anymore explorations on her body and has hung something in front of it; our instructors who, equally fruitless, researched and taught—we ate their fruits long ago, all that has long been eaten, we didn't save them, the fruits, to ensure their continuous supply we had to ingest them, to preserve the *There* and at the same time pervert it, and if too many deny it, we found a new form of *being-there*, and then we firmly ground our origins in our People, very important!, and then we form the core, which isn't a good one, and when we have founded and grounded all of that, we move.

Thank God, here's the photo of the drawing, it's all wrong, that's what we thought all along, it's a totally devious representation, it isn't correct, you'll bite the ground, no, not the ground, the dust in your public-housing home and off you go!, prophet, what's with your call? Why do you call us now?, we have to change cars, the whole thing, not just the tires, it would take forever. Why this call? This house is shaking right now, someone's screaming, we can't even hear ourselves speak, it's the dying who are screaming, no, no one's screaming, really now, they could die a bit more quietly, no, that's not true, there was silence, they were dead right away, why aren't they screaming?, it would be for a good cause! The roof of this building will collapse from all those screams, but that must be another screaming some other place, woe, woe, direct shot through the lung, no, it was the shoulder or whatever, you can read about it later where the shots hit, where and in which body and how often and the suffering in general, how do I lament my friend who is already dead, but was still busily drawing before, always drawing, drawing the unspeakable, unnameable, the unimaginable, we named him, we drew him, we spoke up *and* drew him, that was our mistake, we didn't know who he was or what he looked like, someone who harnesses the horses and then immediately frightens them until they bolt, how does such a one look like? Now that it's too late, we can see that, what did you say?, no idea, oh, here we go moaning again, though mocking was our business, they knocked that out of us as our souls rushed out of our bodies, you can't imagine how they hurried, a bus was waiting already, our souls must be gone, hardly anyone liked them even here. Get rid of them. So there. Now is the time for laments, but no screaming, not here with us, lamenting, it's horrible in there, all dead, the rest of us badly wounded, no more need for a seer to tell us what we should draw and what we should see which way, we know that now: Not like that! We see, we see, yes, now they've opened our eyes, now that it's too late. We should never have seen the prophet, most likely we wouldn't have drawn him either. But we had to behold him, we knew in what high regard he was held, how else could we have drawn him? Supposedly it wasn't even him, too late for the experience, I mean, too late for us to find out now—and how. Now we see him again, we recognize him immediately, too late to draw him. We just didn't have the latest photo, that's not meant as an excuse. Obviously, this drawing is realistic, we made it, from beginning to end, but of course it's not realistic, not even the slightest resemblance, oh horrid, horrid murder! And what for? Just because we've drawn him? We weren't that bad! We are dead and so are our children, our work, our drawings, all dead, we can never do this again.

We would like them to stay alive and only later, at the end, lay down on the ground. The photo is of no use anymore.

That's also a pretty sly way to let us all know what the prophet looks like, and what's more, how he looks now, but the latest doesn't always have to be the correct one either, the way he looks, we could escape him even in our sleep, and we don't give a fuck about what he says, as the bank customer said when he was to pay the anonymous capital-gains tax. In view of the amount he owns, this amount doesn't count, and the names don't get counted either, even though mine is among them. Pity. In view of the crowds he attracts, the prophet counts his income of people credited to him, the interest bites the dust, you can forget it, like people in general. How did they suddenly become so many and the interest so much less?, such inflow and no runoff, no doubt, no one more blessed among people than the prophet, really?, all those people, all at once?, no, it took several times. And he always had that beard, the prophet, fear overcomes these servants, yeah, but also laughter, we want to know if they laughed, no, certainly not, but that's how it's been transmitted to us that many were laughing, just recently the young man in Graz, no idea why, but he mowed people, just mowed them down with his SUV. And did he laugh! Yep, confirmed by citizens who were spared.

Back to our case: Is this really our prophet or is someone playing a joke on us? So we dive right into the room, we unenlightened ones, we don't yet have the new photo but will get it shortly, it plays on every telephone display, it gets played, it is the trump, everyone can have it, it's on its way, the photo, now it's here, too late, our phone already tells us something else again, something more important, a new little game or a song or some other new thing gets announced now and the moment is over, but the photo gets saved for all eternity, right now and forever except if the phone is broken or the battery is dead, which is always just a temporary state. From now to eternity, that's pretty long, that's endless as the Eternal One and exactly as long as his photo can be saved and clicked on again and again, until it doesn't click anymore, that's how long our God will exist. God forever and ever, amen.

We could have waited a little longer, there was a transmission failure, the server broke down, because so many wanted to see their God at long last, yes, the prophet too, we have to wait, but once the photo will finally get here, it will last forever, albeit not indelibly, who'd object to that? No one. Everyone wants it, everyone a different one. But after having waited long enough, we also wanted to see something different for so long. We couldn't wait to add new guilt to the old one and dropped a posting like dung. Well, the Lord said no anyway, no, it's wrong, this drawing is wrong. So what, we already see a totally different one, no one could confuse this one with a man, this one clearly is a naked woman, and there a few pricks are added and that's not a drawing. We sleep a miserable slumber until something awakens us that attracts our attention, are those the photos we've been looking for?, of murdered sons and women?, of burnt people whose relatives weep and weep and scream, in the whole world no more unfortunate ones than they, let's take a look what's next, more photos and films? As a politician, for instance,

you shouldn't have those at all!, it is a revival of people, even
those who have long been dead, that's a beautiful movie, but
the leading actor is no longer alive and we are crying for him,
that man succumbed to drugs, what a pity! Those cartoonists, always useless, even though under constant stress, they
worked so hard to get it right, we put them on the floor now,
but not gently like sleeping people, on the contrary, we, we,
yes, we, we in wild madness's fury, as only Zeus's when he
fathers his sons, because the women don't want to play
along, we floor them. It was all done for you, the muses, the
artists' mistressminds, no, we are saying it was done for our
God and his prophet, they don't fly into such mad fury and
not for what is done with women, that can be quite infuri-
ating, but it's not that kind of fury!

Now you can strike up your Death Song, the mike is held
up to you, start singing, sing about us being inhuman mon-
sters, sing a song dedicated to the God of Night, make a
selfie, but filmed, that's almost the same, only moving, film
yourself killing, then you'll have a nice souvenir of yourself,
except that you'll be dead yourself. It must be captured, that's
the point, just then the murderer breaks away and sees the
door code and pushes, no, pulls, he pushes the door open and
pulls the trigger, no, he lets someone else do the pushing and
just pulls—Oh no!, behold—in front of their father, his children prostrate pitifully before the wretched, what misery!
And the murderer himself has fallen asleep, he takes a rest,
no, he doesn't sleep, after the killing, he does not rest in horrid slumber, neither does he wait for seven days; he must
watch himself on his own telephone with which he filmed
his murders, he must watch the revenges, the advancing

avengers and their unpredictable movements, on this and that station, actually on all stations. We, however—ropes, fetters intertwined—we connect ourselves to this device, talking into it is the least we should be able to do; we don't get away, we must see it all, we've got to watch it. We've got to see ourselves, that's the greatest fun, because we are the lead actors in this series, and our limbs are attached here, can you see? We raise our eyes briefly to the window but keep hearing the ringtone someone wants to talk with, well, it's the signal that was arranged with the device. Now, get to the window, who's there?, is that a bird?, is this a last bird bemoaning the woes of the dead? We wouldn't care, would we not know that we too, though unbemoaned, must leave. No silent old men will be coming now, we know that. Those lying there have been gunned down by us, maybe there are also old men among them, and there is also a woman, no, not this corpse here, that's only one among many, no, the other woman, the veiled wife, a picture of a woman who freed herself from the dress code and put on a bikini, really only that one time, could this be my wife?, that's an outrage, it drives me crazy that this photo exists, getting at something, getting at nothing, so now we'll also wreck what others begot. No tear will be shed because of it; and my wife, my beautiful wife, of course, those artists once again didn't draw a picture of her. Those who believe in God would have seen the beauty themselves, but of course that's not what they draw, no, they've got to draw the prophet! Anything else?

Now someone takes our hero–hands, who's that, no, no one takes our hand and says: My son, what kind of journey is this? And the son says: My God, why have you forsaken me,

I've already said it earlier to the GPS, what has it seen now?, where the street is supposed to be, where it wanted to go, the journey in the car, there is a lake, so here we stand and can't go on; and where a photo was supposed to be a God? Poor guys! Our God has not forsaken us, he tells us his needs, he doesn't need to be shown, at least not shown this way, that's understandable!, crassly distorted, nobody looks like that, let alone a God and probably not even a prophet, whatever, the photo will finally get it straight, but not for us, because of all people it's those who believe in him who don't know what he looks like, the God, the prophet, whoever, their women?, oh God, I beg your pardon, the women are here all right, we have them in stock, but they cannot be drawn either, no image of them, even though it might be worthwhile. So it helps a lot that they can't be seen, they are behind a sort of wall of fabric. How does one get in there? Don't ask me, I might tell you!

We'd pick up levers and axes, we'd kick, hack and lift doors, if we had no better tools, of course also for slaughter and those walls weren't built by Cyclops. Is that Styrofoam behind it? This here, our current residence, is simply a struc-ture, a house, a room, a tea kitchen, a hallway, that's it. And here's already the outside wall. There are drawings of it, there are drawings of everything, and pictures, you can see all of it on the Internet, which keeps everything and at the same time puts it out again, could we look at the originals, yes, I'd say, certainly, the prophet was an original! He must have been one, for none of our pictures of him have been recognized. So he must have been one of a kind, there he stood, like a rock. The pictures are forgeries of something that isn't known. Forgeries of the unconscious, no, of the unknown. This man here says he can free the fire, but he who had the fire didn't permit it. He didn't want to have his work destroyed, of course, fire was supposed to slumber peacefully and wake up only when we need it. The other gentleman—please introduce yourself to the audience in the room and all the visionaries at home with colorful smoke rising in front of them, no, the TV isn't broken, you just think so, because clouds are dancing around in front of you and this other gentleman, our guest today wants the fire to be extinguished only in case of a major conflagration. There's no fire without smoke, no, the other way around, and wherever there is fire, water must never be far away. Yes, it's a short walk, and for an even shorter stretch it will be accompanied by a sense of security. We don't know what the prophet looked like at the time of the drawing of his picture, and we don't want to know. Nonetheless, it sparked a major fire, none of our body fluids, which escape through the holes of the projectiles, will ever extinguish it all. The prophet wants all of this, he wants it this way. He created a fire that man should extinguish with his own water, which he consists of up to 50 per cent, just a moment, I think it's 65 per cent, you can google it yourself and now it's all spilled and out there and you can't get the genie back into the bottle. Well, he must have been an original, this prophet. Still causing this fire so many years after his death! A terrific job! He managed even the much more difficult firestorm. But what else do we have if not our bodies to extinguish fires, and fill them up again with something more refined, with firewater, let's put some fire under our asses, the real spirit, let's look what we've got here. We primordial men have no other way to grasp the outside, even if we had to eat fermented berries—and we'll be happy to do so voluntarily—even animals like them. Everyone, everyone seeks intoxication. And the fire we extinguish ourselves, just with our bodies, but we are allowed to do it with the help of other bodies, we are getting it on and we are putting it out again, with and out of ourselves. The prophet! Well, I have to say! Was that the one who ate locusts? No, not he. We don't even know if he ate anything at all.

Poor devils, they are praying, but they don't know to whom, well, they know that, but not what he looks like and where this countenance will be revealed, which they wrested from incompatibility, no, from incomparability, maybe you don't even like it, this face? Gods, Gods, sorry, God, no, you won't get me to add my name here, they might get me and kill me, they already got one colleague, God, oh God, you reign over evil-doers, you reign over the pious, you protect the law, well, it's your law, you can do with it what you want. A rich filling of gold will go into this tempting cake right under their nose, now how to get it without stealing? So then, stealing! God, you, filled with honors, made of honor, look at them, your people! Why must you confuse all those hearts with your dwindling power, which is a swindle anyway, at least that's what it looks like to me. I beg your pardon once again—no, excuse me—he who rides the chariot of wrongs, shies away from the God's club, your club, yes, yours. Gruesomely wrecked it shall be, your sinister chariot, your sinful consorts shall kick the bucket. Yes, our glistening, expertly expanded roads will win. You won't drift by like smoke, you will produce the smoke yourselves.

Hard to believe, but it's true, it comes from this clear source and from that one too, from newspapers, from pictures posted on the web, the spider has moved out already, it has no room there anymore, too many are fighting against its spin—which proves it is an excellent spin. Billions are praying to him, the One and Only, and yet, they always get by with their will and their work, the believers, who accept as Gods only those of their people, but the One and Only as *the* only one, but what, oh Word, are you telling us herewith? To wit: Have no fear, I won't shut down as of yet, my business remains open whether you like it or not: No common God for everyone, meaning: truly none at all. They know not whereto and for whom and with what, they do not know the prophet but they do know that he is around and that he simply cannot look like that, well, you know, for real, how he possibly might look like. Not like that, gentlemen! Differently, but we are not allowed to know. They ought to be thankful to these artists who do know what the prophet looks like and they show him, that's quite a job which was done almost for free, only this small weekly knows it, anyone can get it for very little money, that's who's got him, and on the front page at that!, a few thousand times, that's too little! For that a few had to perish as well! Instead of being thankful, they kill them, instead of being thankful that they know now what he looks like, that they finally know who they get through to with their questions, should anyone ever listen to them, but they are not getting through to him!, maybe that's why they are so furious, because the network is overloaded, everyone rushes to the phone to admire the prophet and his most faithful followers, everyone wants to see that, the server moans and groans and then it breaks down, they've got the misery of their speculations, but no certainty. And that's what they want to communicate, they want to tell everyone, everyone wants to tell everyone everything, no wonder that the weakest part, the telephone, no, his telephone pastoral caregiver has to die, not to worry, it will work again tomorrow, once the masses have dispersed, because tomorrow everyone will be dying to see something else, immediately!, variety is fun, isn't it? They know it's hard to have a God and a prophet, but who are they? Pray tell! Who are those people? They are not allowed to look at those two and they can't even look at their pictures. You are saying? Then why do they keep doing it? Constantly rousing the pictures from their sweet slumber, denying them their rest which never lasts anyway, because a hand keeps fucking around with them to create a sort of lust and there it pops up, what?, no idea, something pops up, because only that which can be looked at does exist. Now here it comes in handy that no one can do that with the prophet, he can't be looked at, there's no picture and whoever makes one is out and that's that. But supposedly it is not directly forbidden.

The prophet will not stare in shock should he be disturbed, should he be awakened. No one knows where he is. He can't be recognized either. How should anyone be recognized, if there is no picture of him and no picture can be made of him? One should first study the prophet's words before one gets to see him? Isn't this power just a phony power and the house collapses as soon as it stands because it's made of blank cards? Those people turn their faith into a movement without moving, they turn their general cluelessness around and—, around to what? I don't know. They don't have to kill me, it's not worth it, for I know absolutely nothing. I have no idea what they want, but I am covering it quite cleverly, they shouldn't notice that I have no idea, I know the same as you do, I don't know more either, except that they want to murder those poor cartoonists and Jews anyway, you always have to include that in your thinking, it's always playing along, casually, but always, always they always want to kill all those Jews, preferably all of them. They are not even that many, but no, always all of them, for they are one for all and one like all of them. They all stand there as one man, while you stand out as many men, countless men, while their palace has been abandoned, no, attacked, as were their tombstones?, I hope not, whatever happened, I agree with them. They'll get to see who I am. But also the father, everyone needs a father, everyone can use one! But he doesn't make nails with heads, he just knocks them in, the heads. Such destined skill soon gets him to his goal, hands smirched with his own blood, but he also takes strangers. Now he still has to get his own children, but still prefers those of strangers, now he must, with his own hands, transport this blossoming group across the river of death. That's what happens when the father is angry. Should we kill him? He must atone, else human power is all that remains, no more Gods, but humans have also been able to accomplish such feats all on their own! We'll do it again, don't ask me what, it's written right here. Many have tried and didn't succeed. It's been always too few, but now all of them! Let's go! Well then, let's all be Germans! That'll work, but is an effort. First the language must be learned. Forms must be filled out and then they'll most certainly throw us out. They don't welcome so easily, even if we come most well-intentioned, our

being there filled with hardship, thinking filled with danger-
ousness, meaning superfluousness. Yes, this language is
something else! I've long struggled with it to no avail. A curtain tears, a temple collapses, the place where it stood will
never be found again, but God is great nonetheless, he owns
this city, this wall, these people, let's hope he doesn't devour
them for dessert, even though he's had already enough and
afterwards he crushes the house once more into the ground.
That's impossible, because there is no house here. Follow
the signs, then you'll see where it wasn't either.

Germans are born in pain and also die that way, because they
are used to it, oh yes, they do suffer too!, and often at that!,
they have to step over so many who had been pitifully
dumped into the ocean, the desert, stuck into the rivers and
want to get out again, um, do you perhaps mean struck
down? It can be done, it works, like everything does here,
somehow one can get in and among these people, whose
originally offbeat ways of thinking were always miscon-
strued, poor guys, we'll help them extinguish their famous
thinkers who have been on fire for something the same
way—yes, but not really. Once we are in there, it won't be
necessary to confront them with their shortcomings, their
arrogance, their, as they say, excrementations and negation
of community—I think the thinker means their experimen-
tations and addiction to community, because a single person
or a small group could have never committed such crimes.
We'll never disempower them, or the same thing will happen to us, which will probably happen to us anyhow.

What does the Word say? I don't even know what mine says. And if all of us are Germans, we can do anything, we have tried it already, even if not everything, so most of it, it not only works, it sells, it's hot, everyone wants it, everyone wants to be in, everyone gladly accepts it. What won't work at all? It won't work that just out of Godlessness we let a point of view take shape, it won't work to get us in line, we are matchless, we get online to find a match, but who would that be, who knows, not I, all I know is that most people couldn't care less, they don't give a fuck.

Those folks are waiting to find some connection somewhere, it just can't be an outlet, their smartphones are plugged in there already, and since we aren't social beings, we don't have any multi-outlet-power-strips, OK, a power connection, some day they'll be able to do that again, no idea who to whom, but I'll check, maybe I can find a connection, even I should be able to find some kind of connection, how else and, more to the point, why else should I recharge the telephone, which lets me do anything, even make a call? All lines are busy. How else can I find out what to do? Who'd read it or see it? I provide detailed instructions here, but who's interested? I am constantly foaming at the mouth, I am so furious, I shouldn't be, I throw my fury into my face, but I shouldn't do that, for out-of-bounds thinking means staying away from the moment and what else should I say? I already forgot what happened yesterday. I am about to throw a fit, I feel it coming, I have no voice, it's been taken on the last camping trip, no, campaign trail, but I have a sort of cooker, hot-plate, that heats me up, that brings me to a boil, my ears will turn red any moment, is this what they call *menis*, the Greeks, is this the rage of Hercules Furens? Is this *mainomai, furo, insanio*? We would have to briefly turn to the maenads for this, who, however, have turned away from us long ago and migrated into the Berlin club Bergheim—mountain home?, no, Berghain—mountain grove. Does it still exist? No idea, we don't know that about God either, and we don't know how long this furore will last this time, but it is a sensation that's hard to resist, though it has nothing to do with love, rather the opposite. I am numbed by the horror, I can't stop and so I ask: Where am I? My friends are far away for sure, just so they don't have to be near me, no one around to tear me away from my doubts: Is it me raging here? Withdrawn inside herself, but still out of bounds within the narrowest bounds, who heals my forgetting? No forgetting! Never, never again! Yes, I have to keep saying this when I am asked. Actually, I prefer forgetting. Nothing has to get healed then. So I forget, I sink back, but they won't let me, blazing breath now slowly flows out of the lungs, but that'll speed up pretty quickly! Hurry up! Why did my old chest have to be chained to this very column, on which I had put myself before? I am not going to jump down! This column is exactly the place I chose to stay. Only—what am I doing on that mountain top, oh, it's just a pedestal? Am I here in the kingdom of the dead? I hope not. There are people I most definitely would not want to meet. Mommy and daddy, yikes! Everything else familiar has become unhomely, it should be renovated, luckily I still remember my address. Just to be on the safe side, I put a tag around my neck, that's how we managed with daddy. Someone always brought him home. Where I currently am, just to be on the safe side. For my own safety.

I am at sea, as if in a tempest, though I can't really swim, I am in extreme danger then, though not yet dead, in the mind's madness I drop like the cartoonists, a foreign spirit pounced on them that's what they get, drawing people they didn't know anything about, the prophet, whom everyone knows, but they don't want to see him, they keep him in their hearts although he hangs on to their arms and legs like a brick, he hangs with them, so they hang on to him, only with them it causes motionlessness. Death. And death to anyone we bring to him. Should I join a death song now or some other song? I hope not. Oh, I get so angry about the death of these artists, who cares, everybody cares who is angry as well, we'll choose a mild word now, so that they won't kill me too, how should I say?, *orge*?, *ira* in Latin?, I know an Ina, even an Ila, but *menos thymou*?: *animi ardor*, that's it, I found it, don't lie, Elfi, it wasn't you. You sent someone else for it. Have I already mentioned it in another context? Unlikely, at least not with regard to me. Many people are angry who had seen others approach their misery, who were not me—whom they wished such a thing? Quietly I walk further away, no noise, or I—old bag me—might draw attention to myself and that geezer will come back, the one who read my ad, although he is blind, that geezer who can gaze into the future! No, we won't get back to that one now. Lucky them, whoever they are, they can be angry without being me! I would also like to be someone else and, mind you, I'd also like to be younger. I rant and rave and no one notices. My burning breath wrestles its way out of my lung and where does it rise up to?—The ceiling, that's as far as it gets. Could it be because my chest is no longer youthful, my arm no longer strong, oh well, it never was, because I am fettered to the debris of my petrified language which doesn't move, let alone anyone else? You see, this is why I want so much to be younger! Millions of other people can do it! Maybe if I weren't wearing myself out so much? Talk less? That could be it, maybe! I said it already, my language is my column on which I put myself. I am not putting you on! Even though I am unhappy, I am still human! And those cartoonists were human, too! How strange having to specially emphasize this! Oh no, My tears just woke up, now I can't stop them. All dead, all dead. Even a God would cry about this would it befall him. I am so sorry, such pompous word for such an inept speaker!

Could it be because I am already living so close to the kingdom of the dead? That deters people. Understandably so. The thing that always made me hit so hard lies on the floor in form of a Kalashnikov—a form I would have never chosen for my weapon, which I accept nonetheless, since it's not my weapon anyway—so now it lies on the floor, spread all over the ground, because it's me of all people who keeps thinking about why those people had murdered and are dead now themselves. Well, I am certainly not the only one!—what was I thinking?, I am, as usual, one among many, that column, I'll kick it out of the way with both feet, so I can hang directly from the heavens, heaven, I'm in heaven, yes, that's where I come from, why?, because I say so. And my fury, my dear comrade-in-arms, it's always been a great help to me, I get worked up easily and I like it, just as the posters in various forums get worked up easily and they like it too, it's only human—the upshot of home-and uselessness—, they have no one else to listen to them, only this forum listens to them and not too well either, such fury!, well, what about it, can't you say it? You can't or you don't want to? Now it's out of control, my fury, for even though everyone knows not do so, some idiot cut it loose and now the shit has hit the fan. First the grinding of teeth, then yelling, then foot-stamping, then cursing, then bloodlust, bloody fury.

Heracles thinks for a moment: Did it really befall him, his memory fails him, was it a fury? Which one? Folks look at him, the hero and ask themselves if he'd lost his mind, having done so much for them and now being stuck and that's the least they ask themselves. They yell at him: Stay bound until you've calmed down. No wonder he is so furious, with all the misery that befell him! I hear voices. I hear the voices yell at him: We know where your car is parked! Begetter of lies! Your time is running out. You are on the list! What we'll cast into your front yard are stones! You dare putting something on the table that's yourself, you've got balls!, am I seeing things?, now you've put yourself on a pedestal to boot!, this can only be due to your ignorance, I just don't know of what, I mean, I just don't know what you don't know, idiot! Inevitably and unmistakably you have joined the circle of disinformants. This kind of disinformation, which had its heydays in past centuries and these days contributes to the so-called global situation must be dismantled NOW! *Capisce*? Slow down, father, please, I can't keep up, that man spits and foams so much as he talks, is this a detergent ad?, beer?, he is an awful sight, shouldn't I first record it with my smartphone and transcribe it later? I'd prefer it. He rants, he rages, he rages, can't you see it see it, father, we might lose him? It's not enough to lament my destiny, I need a better recording device, I have one but I didn't bring it, I didn't know I would need it. Now he is screaming, he's got this foam at his mouth, which he first has to blow off: You'll never be able to get a good night's sleep again! Well, not if you keep screaming like that. Whatever, no matter how often you censor me with your fascist inquisition key, you'll never be able to stop the truth! My little Goebbels-geek-o-boozer-Matrix-fascist! It makes no sense if you try to bust it, it's my column, my bust's on it, I'll bust myself, if need be—and it's quite hard, believe you me! You'll find out what your feet will have to say about it. How should I respond to that? Not to what your feet have told you. Either you wake up for real or you remain in your station—as a bringer of lies! Lies! Lies Lies Lies! So then why don't you say something when you are in better command of the truth!

All right. I'll talk, but not before you got rid of this bloodlust, I've said it before, but in your bloody fog you didn't hear it. Loser and parasite! If you were really such a genius in your field, you'd have gotten a decent job, but you didn't. So get yourself a blow job from a welfare whore in case you ever get a hard-on. Well, if that whore got in, we'll get in too. We are coming, we'll just have to pull the Sun God's arrows out of there, so we can use them again and then we're coming. Did you really think, this would have no consequences for you? You'll never have a good night's sleep again! WE know where you live, WE know your face. Dress warmly. Sparks will fly! No matter how often you'll censor with your Fascist-Inquisition key, you'll never be able to stop the truth! These are not words of a riddle.

Let's put them together, the thinker's words, how physics could never imagine them, which *follows after the beginning*, before the world takes on its shape and still prefers not to shape up, because everybody is always in such a rage, it closed their mind, and even my fury no longer raises an eyebrow, it gets presented as a has-lost-it thing, but no one's looking. Anyone disempowered that way first gets angry, then asks who turned off the power and then throws a fit. Anyone who's got a problem finds a repairman and that is usually God, yes, but which one? You've got the right address, here things get done un-bureaucratically, and so that's the one we join, sometimes it only takes two or three weeks and already we have joined something, we had no way to know. All the better. It tears doubts apart: That's fury! We've got it, we grasped it and now we can't grasp what we cooked up here: I wouldn't call it a meal. That's how fury puts it, it puts you in a daze and you don't know what you are doing, but you keep doing it nonetheless. I don't know now where I am. I don't know who my friends are and where they are, far away or close, better far away, otherwise I might kill them too and then I'd have no more friends, that would be a shame, wouldn't it? Who is far away, who is close by? That one's far out, I don't know anyone who talks like that: *Feierabendbierchen*—after-work-beer?—chemical slurry-natrium-glutamate-chemical crap-fast food. Pharma-Mafia-vampyre-chemical crap like fluoride in toothpaste and aluminium on the head or in deo, no, in her, or nanoparticle in idiot-Pandemrix-pig-piss-flue-shots and DAX-pusher-matrix-blue Viagra pill-fodder next to—sure thing!—nuclear-war-monger-aspartame-chemical slurry-soft-drink soda. Mind fuck! Microwave toaster! Boob tube for homeland-securitynarco-hypnosis! Thoughtless, thankless, thriftless! Before, mind and body still in good health, then consumed every imaginable industrial toxics from the supermarket shelves, contaminated I wanted to say, consumed the contaminated, well, where is it now—healthy common sense, where's your critical academic-analysis-know-how, shoved up your ass? Is it anal? Is it banal? I say with absolute certainty: Yes! Do you think we can untether him now? Might he have tied himself up there? I don't know why people always have to tie themselves in knots and then go stark-raving mad about it! Unbelievable! Well, I can believe it.

In my fury I can't tell the difference between any of this, I just thrash around blindly, blindness is key to fury, sometimes it's difficult to produce it, it's not an industrial mass product, it has to be made individually. Then a catastrophe has to be reported and then we are amazed how people can rage like this. They ignore their limitations. What, and I'm supposed to have killed my wife in such a state? I—my wife's murderer? That's not possible! Oh, yes, my son, good thing you ask, I happen to know that you did it all by your own hand, though you did have to add the second hand. What, really?, my wife? I didn't want to kill her, I wanted to wreck the whole house but didn't notice that she was in there! You don't notice anything in such a state. The one who could have torn me from my doubt hasn't been born yet, fury knows no doubt, there is no time for it, second thoughts come first, if at all, it's too late afterwards—who'll heal my forgetting? No one, for I don't want to forget, I want to let it all out, all the things I never knew, there it runs, the unconscious! Like those men I am also incredibly mad at, but in my blindness I can't see, are they the guys we wanted to kill? I can see the trigger and I know how to use it and what's going to happen, but still, we ask ourselves, where did such fury get a hold of us? Where did such raging come from and become all the rage? Where was it? Where did it ruin us? Whose ruin did we bring about?

The difference between the raging Hercules and ourselves is that our questions reached somebody who gave us the answer that related the hidden truth, it had such power that language could not keep up with it, it dribbles out of our mouth, it ends up—after much spitting, cursing and raging— this now-exhausted language ends up in a bubble of talk about things which don't exist, because it got tired and doesn't have much more to say. You can see it right here. Snot! Snot! We were told and it got done. The glow that emanates from the prophet is just another bubble, which he is not, he doesn't appear, it just appears that way and if you don't believe it, then your number is up too, so then the appearance only confirms—though only for those in the know, for us, only for us and one and a half million others— our very own, most essential *being*. So you see, this is why we do it. This is why we work so hard at it.

I think this is it—letting something out which has never been in there. It creates a sort of vacuum no vacuum cleaner can manage—who wrests doubt from me? Not necessary. Who heals my forgetting? Not necessary. For everything familiar has become unknown to me. Oh well. No wonder the Gods have left even Greece, after they'd withdrawn all their money from the banks, so there isn't much left to get out of them, so they must get out themselves. Now they are spent as well, the Gods! There they go, elementary-school teachers gone crazy, idiots who never were taught anything, unemployed technicians who don't understand the essence of technology but are experts in applying it, the last of the sinking middle class who has been dumped by the last bank. Fatherless sons, I could tell you a lot about those, but I'll spare you. Or I'll get back to them, when the foam has flown off my jaws and the snot off my nose, and this will take a while, I am eating just now. There they go, those guys, and they do know what they're doing, their thumbs hammering away. My God, they are already totally deformed, those poor thumbs, but it was worth it, it was worth being able to text yet another message.

But no, that's just the beginning, please don't start screaming again, it wouldn't do you any good, you may only get into your car when all this is over, really all over, it will last exactly as long as I want to. They are not too lowly for us, those cartoonists, we want to add, they are not to be underestimated, OK, maybe by others, but we, we actually hold them in high esteem, they are worth every death there is. They will no longer insult anyone, we prevented it our way, which finally showed them our estimation. With the precision of our choices and decisions, we decided on a couple of artists. No arm reaches out against it, we've got enough arms to take them all out, whether spotted predatress of the fields or men in jeans, plus one piece of woman, but she doesn't count anyway, not for us, there hardly is any talk of her. And she didn't even draw. We mow them down in the grove they fled to with their stupid pencils. Such small pencils and creating such nonsense. That's all they know, that's all they can do.

That's nothing, they don't slaughter anyone and whomever they skewer, they forget again quickly. Pencils and their mourning kin, sharpeners, sharpies, harpies. And yet, shame lives far from their Goddess, Violence, so we feel no shame either, we are the strangers' murderers, whom we don't understand, well, we do understand the murderers, that's us, duh!, we even understand those strangers, they skewered our God, we saw it right away and understood it, and now they've been removed, we slew them and that includes all modes of death, there weren't so many options in antiquity, right? They also paved the way for other mockers, but those know better now, they wouldn't dare to come out of their cubicles where they locked themselves up in airless darkness, for this is how these people live, never out in the fresh air, always just drawing in their dens, their offices, even in their pockets, always just the pencil, which pops open like vacci-nated tissue, in their coat pockets or elsewhere, which opens like an injection's scar, which no longer happens either, since the respective illness has been wiped out, eradicated. The scars disappear, but not the bills. Accounts must be settled and we take care of that. And death, the River of Death, is the goal of our labor. Let their house mourn, let it mourn, other houses mourn too, many might mourn, but those here, they won't return, maybe others will, who have also drawn an unfortunate lot, but not those, we blocked their way. The boat has already been rigged, we rigged it well— but no more buckaroos for buccaneers this year, yeahyeah, be annoyed!,—and now it's going down with them and soon also with all those, who go in for them, take it from me! We'll get them all! We'll get you!

We consult the book of our youth, for we are forever young, that's for sure, and naturally different stuff is printed there than in the book of geezers, yes, we've got different stuff to read, which helps us kill the time to Hades's house. We can do anything, we are swinging the weapons, we run up the staircases and then down again, we jump into cars. We are the children no one gave a shit about and who don't give a shit about anyone. Let them wipe their own asses. Let them get a real toilet. Children without a father and mother, both dead, now what? A killer career! Now look here, no madman can pull this off, fury won't do it. Reason's the rule here, responsibility, not Goddesses of madness and night, with snakes in their hair and whips in their hands.

Madness shows humans their limits so that they can surmount them and that's where the fun starts. But those are not madmen talking, well, maybe one woman, here barriers get moved around to put the killers in their place, further and further to the back, but the killers can always be seen much better up front, that's paradoxical, move immediately behind your barriers. No, no, we won't do that. And we are certainly not mad. We love those barriers, so that we can ignore them, it's anger rather than fury, that's what it is, I beg your pardon for not explaining this in more detail, I am not begging too loudly, I know, you already feel sorry for us, but even more so for yourself for having to listen to this. Should I send a messenger to whom you could talk?, free of charge, of course, she has no medical or psychiatric training, but talk to her anyway, you hero—who had tasks assigned to him and executed them all, and now he infects nice people with madness to boot, the closer they are to him the madder he gets. That's because the hero didn't let himself be put in his place, which we had moved further back, especially for him, where he would've hardly been seen and we wouldn't have become jealous. No one would have seen what he did. He could have hidden himself in the house. Someone was still lying there, his eyes darkened by night, he could have killed him too. He doesn't want to. So, that settles that, no, stop, behold! Behold!, he does after all! It would never occur to him that he'd have to atone for the bloodguilt. And he won't have to. He has long been due to die, but he doesn't want to. He wants to die, but on his terms, flee, flee, all of you, as long as you are still able to! And all those honors for these cartoonists and those dead Jews!, so much honor, too much honor for sure, I can't yet see the end of it, the end of my patience, however, I can see it coming, so take yours and get out of here, if this gets too boring for you! The hero shines in heaven and on earth, you bet!, that's a fact, he brought peace to rugged land and raging sea. But those men do the opposite. They are the blasphemers who undermine peace and mine it for all its worth, and throw as many bodies as possible into the hole so that all the digging—which the hero did huffing and puffing like crazy, because it was so much work and no one helped him—would pay off.

I advise them to stop considering such horrors, but they completely misjudge the situation. You'll never be allowed to call yourself a hero, even if you'd kill your mother and father like this good man here, oh, if only I could be in his place! It wouldn't do me any good, I'd have missed this opportunity. He, on the other hand, he kills wife and children, this has happened many times, just that the killers did not have to fulfil as many tasks before, they weren't robbed of as many years of their lives, on the contrary, they were spared their lives, such precious gift!, well, maybe not so precious, it was thrown to them like a bag of dirty laundry for mother to wash, so they wouldn't get their hands dirty.

Don't know who that is and that one there, they don't look familiar. I have a brother and both of us have adoptive fathers like this hero. His real father is dead, actually he was a God, but no one believes us as usual. The family gathers to give thanks and then this madman who had worked so hard before!, who'd been robbed of years of his life by difficult labor which is now finished because he is dead, no, he is not!, so this maniac kills them all and declares that he only did it because they wanted to kill him. A common excuse of murderers. I killed him, yes, because he wanted to kill me first. Besides, it was an honest fight. Besides, it was an accident. The furious swing their empty hands, those of the angry ones' are full, because they brought all their weapons. The furious ones have their weapons attached to them already, the angry ones have to first buy or get them, and that kind of video stick also comes in handy, so they bring it, it goes into a small frame which then gets mounted on the head or wherever they want to, whatever extremity which, however, should be out in the open, and raised as much as possible, so one can look down on all the others, yes, so that's where it gets mounted, right, and then it can see everything, it can see exactly what we can also see, that's its limitation, it doesn't see beyond us, beyond itself it does. It can see but it has to leave everything as is, because we handle the rest. The furious one has nothing at hand, he just has his hand, the hero is the weapon, beware when he's given a free hand! Then he lets the weapon rage! The angry one plans ahead, the furious one goes ahead and kills. Poor devil!

The blood drips from his hand. The angry one would wash his hands now, the furious one pays no attention to something like that. He doesn't care how he looks, though he does pay attention to his clothes—black and dangerous and the spots not too visible; and the flag, he's got that too for sure, he always has it with him; I am still breathing and see what I am supposed to see, what they let me see, with pleasure at that, well, yes, he wants to look good, later, when he's dead and, before that, on TV, while he is already in the process of leaving the living. He jumps out of the car when no one sees him and strides and steers with empty hands, the weapon still hanging in his belt, he always has it with him, it is him, he is the weapon, it is like he is, always ready, but understanding: Nothing. *Nix verstehn.* He makes gestures as if he were swinging a scourge, we, the subordinates find him ludicrous, we can't even imagine such a thing, but we'll soon see it in the special prophesy, the special program, his own action cam will even broadcast it personally, so we can be there too; somehow ridiculous, man in his fury, it's easier to understand the angry one, he has grounds to live on comfortably, causes he is attached to, effects fucked up long before he is done, but none the less: ludicrous and horrific all at once can only be the furious, like the little furry, no, fury-friend here on this rock, not a shepherd, we are the shepherds!, the one with the bleeding eyes, yes, the one who almost lost the light from being blinded, he wasn't blinded by himself, up on the rock, he had been blinded, the raging guarantor who got nothing back for himself, only pain, one who was almost hit over the head by the eaves dropping all around him, it's awfully loud, his neighbors also wanted to hear what he had to say and then they want to say it too, much louder, of course, something that was yelled at him. The *forethrown*—and by that term I don't mean the forebears, they rather walked, those thrown are the furious, yes, they are ahead of us. The furious one is always offside, he kills, because he is not grounded, he sees no grounds for checking how far he can go, it depends on the opponent, whom he picked himself and when he is and remains by himself he is especially dangerous. You can't refer to him, you fatherless murderer, for fatherlessness is about all you have in common with him and all of you did have nice adoptive fathers, well, not all, but most, and this must also be said for once.

Everyone is entitled to have a father, but not everyone has one. Often the father is dead, thus violating the norm of producing still more sons and subsequently lecture them for ever and ever. But of course he can also delegate all this to another authority, which is supposed to reinforce the implacability of the law and that happens frequently, just think of Oedipus— all the things he could still have done without a law!, yes, he was something else!, he was a man! Always already blinded by himself, but blaming others! Sadly, this authority is a total failure. It undermines, demeans the demented father—who would have had parental authority, but was no longer competent, which we regret—or denies him altogether. But still, it gets paid by the father, who doesn't want to bother with the sons. The father pays so that the police, the ambulance and the fire department can function, and he also pays for the roads used by these authorized vehicles. He wants to be free. He doesn't want to have this madman in the family. He begot him, but then he didn't want what he got and then he demolished the entire office of Children and Family Services. This, unfortunately, made the son go mad, but maybe there were also other reasons. How come you know all this? How did you hear about it and from whom? Now look, such a delirious activity comes to light also in the form of images copied from role models who don't even want such an image, not a smart thing to do. Now it looks even less becoming. Some things are better kept in the dark. Everything is distorted, yes, here too, the picture totally distorted, no one disappeared, I mean to the distant land, inaccessible to our steps, war reigns there and soon it will reign here too. Folks are always moving there because they have something important to do there. They don't say what.

And for those staying at home: Folks who had nothing better to do than drawing ugly pictures are just getting slaughtered and left lying wherever they dropped, they weren't even eaten, that would've made some sense at least. We, however, we also were entitled to a norm-setting father, we would have had the right to one, but we didn't have any, father I mean, so we don't have norms anymore. The father's authority was badly hurt, he was taken from us, OK, so now we take what we can get, for example the lives of strange people whom we don't own. What's written below this photo? It says: born to a father, and because we couldn't remember our births to save our lives, no, that part comes later, we turn against this father who represents the public, while mom still prefers staying at home, she works part-time, instead of getting fucked by flex hours, or she is dead, for us in any case, she has died for us. We turn against the father who is more important, and by doing so, against the public and against this and that norm which we don't even want to get to know, and against everything that still has some kind of rationality.

By killing, we turn against this sucking Nothing, that would be our father, who every one of us is entitled to, so we can fight him, so he'll come with us and stay true to the suffering that is inflicted on us, but we don't have one. Through these killings we want to assert our claim, even if it's wrong! Herewith, we file the claim. The Christians and the Jews wear our father's face, which is a fake, not his face, no one has faced him face to face, which they don't face up to, sad, but true. Not everyone can face his face, and that's a fact. That's why he wants another one. We have a father who has no face, therefore anyone can be it.

So our father must not be depicted, so we don't know what he could have looked like, no, we don't, so we can see him as the greatest of all, no one can check it. OK, you will be killed shortly, you must be killed, or else we can't get control over you, and someone has to fill this gap. Not a father—well, we, we don't have one. By dying, we submit to the ordinance of our origins. There might be others who got off to an even worse start, but those rather turn away in tears from their sons than the other way around. The sons break with their fathers, that's why we have them, but there is none far and wide. There is a gap, a hole, where the father should actually be. Our father who art. Our father would have been like Heracles, even better: Heracles himself: not to be stopped by anything. If you think we'll flee now, think again. Kill them all. That's not how it was in the old days, that's how it is today; in antiquity, no one would have thought of it, not even a poet. Please, said this girl, can you kill me without hurting me?, that would be nice. The neighbor says yes, I can, grabs her by the arms and pulls her outside. People tell him, they yell at him, that she is pregnant, that girl. I don't mind, says the neighbor and slits open her belly with his machete. He takes his time and opens it very carefully, like opening a purse. That's how some humans do it, not even a God would have had such an idea, he knows how much work it is—producing humans. He sure knows. Kill them all, also my most loved ones, yes, and the neighbors too, with pleasure, that's a fact and we don't even know those cartoonists as of yet.

The problem is, as usual, that no one loves us, no one holds us dear and if there is any limit to suffering we don't know it. There are no metrics for suffering. Surely, measurements would have to be taken beforehand, so one could orientate oneself, but there are no standards, we have lost all sense of proportion. We fall outside the order of the world, but the world has never been able to keep order. No one is to blame.

It cannot be said: Where am I? Well, it can be said, go ahead, well, doesn't anyone tell him where he is? Who? Man is never where we look for him, says the thinker, this religion even offers him to also include himself in its history as man among men, with all those dead ones it's no big deal, what do you think? Tell us. As the last residue of living matter? That may well be, their residues will be around for a long time, or will it be their representations?, no, that wouldn't be enough, those aren't images, it's really them, so much life has never been captured in any device! Someone just killing his family, even though he doesn't know what that is and where and most of all, who they are, mother and children, that's also because of this terrible fatherlessness, but in this case the father is the one left! What's left for him to do other than heading towards great suffering? But first he must find them, the mother, the sons. He'll find them, I am not worried. He found the Hydra, the lion, the boar, the vultures, the bull and I don't know what else, he should be able to find his own children and spouse! We already told you about the club, and how he kills his children, the one about the Kalashnikov I have been trying to tell you all along, but I can do this only in words that befit common folks and those are below me.

OK, here we go: I am copying the instructions for the automatic gun, but I can't envision it. The murder, yes, but not the device. Is this the language of a murderer who has endured so much and can't get enough of it? Is this the talk of the furious, of the fanatic, the possessed, the psychopath who is out of control?, because at the moment he has lost it, he isn't even able to talk. He can't put anything on its feet anymore, not even himself. Wait a minute, I'll take a look, the three-headed dog is also looking, he is irritated, animals feel things before people do, he just doesn't know which head he should bite with. No, the hero's lost his head, gone to the dog?, no, sorry, doggone lost it, though the deed is still his to account for. There are witnesses. The child hugs the father and says: I am your son, don't you remember? Doesn't matter. Away with you. The third child, did we forget the second? Dead too, sure enough. He chases the children with their mother around the altar, you remember what I said before?, good, because I don't. Delusion can't be cured, it does not let the patient suffering from this disease find any other victims, it has to be the most loved ones and we don't yet even know those cartoonists, well, not personally, so take them out, right now! That's how the furious sees it, it's an individual eye, not everyone can do it and, luckily, not everyone does it, except to mom and dad whose severed, dripping heads are carried around, it is not immaterial who did it, they are the ones who do it, because they are absolutely mad, the others gain a certain clarity by doing it.

Everything's ridiculous when you think about death or something like that—one can say this about absolutely everything, the poet has also asserted it, though he actually asserts himself by saying it. OK. And the third child and the woman, its mother are killed with one single arrow. Why waste two? It's relatively easy to get someone off his rocker to pass out, if not on. You walk over to him, provided, of course, you can get near him, and throw a big stone at his head, he drops, subito, just in time, actually too late but at least at long last! He loses consciousness. Father, he no longer can say the word and he isn't one anymore because his three children are dead. I think he left one over. Otherwise, all over.

The father, actually the foster father like Joseph, both saviors, one gentle, the other furious, are both sons of non-existent persons who nevertheless represent the existent to the extreme, sons of Gods, whose fathers, God, Zeus, all of them Gods, why not, when there were still several, when Greece was still what it used to be, so let's take that one, all Gods anyway, who somehow, despite the adjusted border-lines that had been drawn for them are doing something we don't like most of the time but they do, well, they aren't doing it with us, we don't count, so much gets moved around, borders moved so far back they almost disappear in the evening fog and yet they are there, you just know it, but can't see them, so that the Gods can get across—so that they can get over it, they cross the line in one jump, that's why they became Gods, but not for us, that's where they draw the line, I mean, before we could get anything across to them they had already crossed us off. They come when they are least expected, what for do we need borders if they are not observed, and not just by God—this one and that one and also the one in-between? They are getting to us somehow, they keep landing here non-stop, they decided in secret and we have to take the shit for it, we are the ones getting stabbed in the bathroom, shot in editing rooms, in super-markets, no, it's not us yet, I just see, it's others. The Gods are coming and then they blame us, even though it wasn't us. And clueless about how to even recognize living matter. In order to find us without having to slaughter us right away—how should we know how they'll decide, those Gods?—they revert to their most grinding flaw, that is, having no ground to stand on, the ground lies in the original form, which will now be abandoned, so that no more of our species can be made. (Brush up your Heidegger, I told you so!), Why do they create us if they don't want us to reach our goal and end? Why did we remain just drafts, dear Gods?, so that you can throw us about? So you can draft us to kill? So that horrific stuff inside us can reveal itself? If you hadn't shown it to us, we couldn't have thrown ourselves at each other on top of it, we wouldn't have had anything but us and we couldn't have empowered ourselves either. They do their job, the little Goddies, those Godlets, and we are supposed to obey them, but we only follow our own lordi-dada, and besides him there is no other one, everything that's written here is invalid, forget it! Now you are relieved, I can see that. Why did you work so hard to follow me? You didn't even do it, I am in a totally different place. And where are you? Until I found out that it's rightfully here, but what exactly is it?, I forgot, but you, you can remember it again. God says, the generations must be kept separate and in cages, so that they would not intermix disastrously. Mind you, reason and madness have to keep at least one step apart! They take care of law and order, the Gods, not ours, he takes care of us, he takes care only of us, but the others stand on legal grounds, which are groundless, except that they say what's what, and how often it can happen so that we can get away with it. (You've got to dig deep here into the thinker's ground.) What are you saying, daddy, did you wake up? Oh, I almost forgot, you prohibit murder, and murderous actions, shit, we should have read that sooner or known about it somehow, since we torched the library in our neighborhood and your mail reached us just now, we didn't check. Oh dear, we should have known that you don't want murder. At the most one can say: I could kill so-and-so. But it must not be done.

Look here, you've never seen anything like it: Our action and
the language are separating now, even though we are still
using our smartphones, I have no idea and I don't want to
know it, but they could still make calls, the murderers, I
think, the third one could still shoot his little movie and even
send it, otherwise the audience might have thought someone else had killed the Jews, the Germans did it again, no,
not this time, we can prove it. Action and language are stepping apart, they split up, but there is no doubt that it was us,
we insist on it and there is enough footage, which can't run
away again. For this is how technology works: What's here
must also stay here. That's all that counts, that we stay here
and prove we are not just a mob, we can do our job. Had we
had a daddy, not just an adoptive father—the one of Heracles, for example, gets saved the last moment, the Godfather,
no, the foster father, was saved, isn't that swell, but then he
wasn't the real thing, he was not the yellow of the egg, as
we say here and, no, not the heidegg, nothing came out of
that one!, so if we had a real daddy and not this surrogate,
who doesn't even have to be killed, he doesn't count, he
didn't conceive us, he is a nothing as opposed to his sons, he
could have saved our victims from extinction. If daddy
wouldn't have allowed it, we wouldn't have killed them,
that's a no-brainer.

OK, let's hear our fate and let others have it, so we don't have
to take the shit. We are missionaries, no, and I won't make
the joke about this position now, that would have been the
last one I haven't made already. And lightless the hero's
rolling in his chains this father put him in, so that he, the
hero would not kill him, the father to boot, I wouldn't put

it past him, this son of a God, one sacrifices himself, the other all others, simple as that. A word and a blow.

That's the difference, cheers the Word, which all of them believe, which all of them trust, without knowing it, well, someone will know it, one with whom the Word *is*, in the beginning was the Word and where did it go this time? But the one who knew better, though not a better word, had been knocked out and chained, even though there were no more children left to kill. Well, just one, one more to go. As a pop analyst, I say—no, that's not me—well, so what: When the narcissistic wound of not having had a father gets too powerful—and it doesn't help that daddy was a real God—, then we, the fathers will kill our own sons, they shouldn't have it better than us. Period. But the father is still around, I mean the father's father, he is one too, that's often forgotten that many are a father, who have to master plans, which will find another master. Yes, indeed, this father chained his son so that he wouldn't kill him too, the son the father who isn't even his father, he only adopted him. He took on the son but didn't pass on his rules, he still needed his ruler to measure the doors of the palace and the windows, the latter because of curtains, not to curtail the horror in there. Those children won't cry anymore, we took care of them, the hero killed them, stupidly, they were his own. We already explained this to those born after, who will never see the light of day, because now there were only two balls in the air, and they were bouncing against each other, and then one dropped, do I mean now this ball or the other? I don't know, they look so much alike. Yes, fury fries the brain, it can't think anymore, anger sharpens it, one can plan ahead and prepare. Though the result is always the same. Exactly. What's left is lying right here. I hope you possess the precious gift of hearing. I don't. I don't need it anymore. I only have to write this, I no longer play the violin, not even the viola, but you, poor you, you have to listen to this, I wouldn't want to be you but, rather, chain you to a column so you can't ever leave from here, well, I wouldn't really go that far.

Yes, pile up heavens on your shoulders like water, before it surrounds you completely, oh God, is that cold, luckily I prevented a heart attack by getting gradually used to the water!, it's better that way—first splashing yourself with a bit of heaven, since you will never get there, heaven is all booked, the Gods have bunkered down there themselves, the tables are laden and the foster fathers work their asses off during the day, you dear foster fathers, I feel so sorry for you, the way you pull and tug at us and hold up high your qualification certificates! You are blind toward the deeds of your sons, but the blindest are the sons of Gods, that is, at the very least they are as blind as the fathers, but one cannot be least blind, it's either or.

They tell me, after all those hours, that now I must get a ranking or the ski champion will surpass me if she is judged only by time. It is a matter of one-hundredths of seconds. So, there we have two, no, actually three, we already had the two murderers of the cartoonists, didn't we, no, hold it, here we have three sons, two adoptive fathers, the third I am not sure about and was too lazy to read his bio; not one for each of the sons, but Joseph, the foster father, who had to foster the son of that God after he had received him directly from this heavenly father. God lets his son die, that means nothing else than: he kills him, he sacrifices him for the whole of mankind, while the other sons would rather sacrifice the whole of mankind, with the exception, of course, of all their loved ones their heart is beating for, no, they've got no heart, but several cars, though in the end only two, in which they beat it, but then botched it, the cars would have liked to drive on, with pleasure at that and they'll do it again, they will be repeat offenders, serial fender benders, even though a gas station played a dirty trick on them, by which they were recognized, but the drivers, who'd also like to do it again, those are dead, you bet!, the gas station also had a part in that. They all keep saying, it's the fucking oil, no, not something that crude, and it isn't crude oil they put in cars.

Who we are? It doesn't seem necessary to know, it is enough to know we are, that keeps us plenty busy. But we could also be these actors, what is a human?, an actor, meaning a value-setting animal that runs along or away in a movie?, stop! Or are we, these actors only a husk for the author's soul that's floating away into some eternity while she is busting her ass right now? How can we present ourselves in a way that'll get us to be talked about because we talked about something completely different? Or are we the only site—no, surely not the only one, we love to tour other sites, so that we can be guests somewhere—are we one of the many sites of the truth of being and the connection to being? Say what? Pa-lease, will you finally let go of that stupid book which you have dug yourself into for years, you dumb cow, you don't understand it anyway! Just be yourself—yawn—go ahead, if you don't do it now, you'll never find back into your self again, and who would want to find you anyway? Right: We are only our own truth and all those other truths—we're just acting them, no idea as what or in what role, as long as it is big enough, the role, for even toilet paper has or is only one roll, at least a small one, no? I see, this man in the first row starts to have a fit. Avoid him when he rushes out, move a few seats away from him, in case you even got a ticket, which I take it is a given for this play.

Night's ghost, be gone! Relentlessly writing away here is a nice lady, even though she often is called other names, she lets you have it, she lets all of you have it, though not for free, but she hands it over, so that she can shine in her uniqueness, with that woman you will even save battery space, I can assure you, that glowing beam which she would like to screw herself into, which she would like to screw on, indicates how far she is still charged up, this pitiful raging, moaning woman, oh!, I!, without a doubt, this is me! Anyway, she looks like me, her star will soon be extinguished or covered up, outshone by others. She preaches wisdom, look at me, you'll see right away that I am preaching. But taking action for once? No way! She always knows it all before. Even the sun knows what I hate, I'm telling you too, I have to submit to another's will. They want me to tear open my breast and finally shut up, they do *not* want me, no matter what, to come out, leap out of my marble palace, which I don't have, into the unknown, eek!, I'm not doing that and, besides, this is only a single-family house, so I don't have to get out of my family home, I would never do that anyway. I should stay where I am, otherwise I might murder children, which I don't have. I shake out my hair, which I dyed and

blow-dried yesterday, I role my starry eyes, which are covered with computer specs at the moment, I need others in
another place, and for the big distance in which I mostly find
myself, still others, glasses for farsightedness for my far-out
self, I growl, I get ready to jump, but then I just walk up and
down the stairs of the single-family house. No, I don't teach
anyone this dance, because the music always plays some
other place, I should float—to Mount Olympus, instead, I
just sneak into this house and stay there. I feel so sorry for
people, but what can I do, because: No one remains unhurt
by fate, not even God remained unhurt, but he at least had
the choice, at least ours did, didn't he, I don't know about
the other but speak enthusiastically of him, I must say I am
thrilled about him, but not about his followers, exactly as
suggested by our avatars in the abysses, the fords of the fora.

Nonsense, where was I, not even our God remained unhurt
by fate, which he chose, in the meantime we have been told
that he died for us, well, as far as I am concerned, he could
have also stayed alive, but then what would have happened
to his beautiful religion? Jesus Christ on a stick!, well, since
I already started the sentence before and then forgot it again,
hold it!, here it comes again: God doesn't lie, except Zeus,
who constantly lies to his wife; and the half-blind singer; as
for myself, I don't lie either as far as I know and that's not
much. I get into a fight with every man, preferably father, I
fight with everyone, but for power, I don't just punch someone in the face. Everything must have its grounds. What I
am saying is on most solid ground. Only, I can't find it. I am
touching for it with my feet, could it be I am floating?, no,
that cannot be. So then, in order to reach it, I would have to

dive deep down, but I can hardly keep myself on the surface, a couple of strokes and I am tired already.

Or, no, let's put it that way, how I—referred to as *we* in what follows because I can't bear being alone with me—I always say *we*, so then, how we could have never said it: Knowing who we are is so absolutely necessary, that without this knowledge we can never say for sure whether we really *are* or just arrange ourselves in *non-being*, and take ourselves as *being*, because we *think*, that is we *are*.And there are people who can't even bear this, not thinking and not being. Neither one. The murderers, those worthless animals as opposed to a human being, who, nonetheless, is also an animal but one who sets values and then bargains forever over the price, so what are they doing? This one goes home so that he can get out of his clothes, he is covered with blood. Those two murderers got themselves unbelievably filthy. Should Islam believe in the soul—I am intentionally not looking this up now, so that I cannot be punished, I pretend ignorance to prevent getting into trouble—then he can now watch his soul flying away, floating into eternity where the virgins are waiting for him, and if it is a virgin who blows someone up, then she may get married in eternity, then she can even set up a second person in relationship to her *being*, and that one sets up another one and that one another, this is how the chain of command for women works there, some day she'll have to catch on! Isn't it a hoot what's expecting her there. Now those two murderers have sighed out their lives and the two girls too, who had courageously put themselves in a full-body garment so they couldn't be seen at all in their wrapping, they sighed something and then they went on a trip, who knows where those two are, maybe they aren't dead yet. In the meantime, another one popped up in Denmark, whoever it was, I don't get to the end of all those highly praised cities, where people should be warned by travel agencies, rather than seen dead or in horrible condition, a mistake, they should all be dead, then it would all be over and done with and I won't check either if they were married. Most of them were, if only briefly, that's why they went there to begin with, they are entitled and then they did return the wife again, used, but not used up, something was still left, they passed her on, according to custom. I know for sure only with regard to the supermarket killer, but I am not going to check now if the other two were married as well. I mean, I won't open anything, I won't drag anything out of nowhere onto the screen, where I could read up on such a conspicuous detail. I am intentionally not doing this, someone has to evolve out of all those intentionally evil deeds, no, not I, someone without any intentions, who is not dizzily addicted to all the news, who has as little interest in the old as in the new. Like me. Exactly.

Those two are resting well now in their self-certainty, they lie there for eternity, the third one a bit later but for sure, but I stop it with him, right now, whoever comes next, anyone pushing himself, as of this moment, into this moral tableau cannot be painted anymore, there is no more room, it's all far too long, as usual and I can't get a grip on all this anymore, well, maybe I can, but not here. But one must also consider why these people are doing this, I follow them like a Goddess of a highly praised city, let's see who's turn is next, I really think: London, but those already had a turn of terror, blood and screams, often fruitless screaming, would any town go for it voluntarily?, certainly not, what are you thinking? Where is that going to get us, I don't think at all, let alone of getting somewhere, I hardly get out of my apartment, where I wash my hand of any sinful guilt, which I wasn't able to take on anyway, for lack of opportunity, I am really free of sin, believe it or not, my God believes it, for he can see it: You finally found a place for it, and now you don't want to keep it! You want to trade places? Too late. So, now I'll throw the first stone, I was already looking forward to it, I can do that, I can write a political drama, even though it isn't dramatic, even though you won't find anything political, well, maybe that, but definitely not a drama, I am supposed to write the inside of characters, why they did it, right?, why and how many, as to that city, I won't wash my hands but yours and imagine that I freed her from a steer, no, even better, of all those gross boars, I'd also settle for a bear—who, come to think of it, isn't doing so well these days, is he?,—from all of those, who crowd and cloud her over, the city, what am I compared to her, a Nothing! And as to the fields of my active presence, I myself assigned all of those to me, I keep saying *we*, but that's not me, I am not any of them, neither am I the refugees who are talking here, how could I be a refugee, I can't even escape to a movie or a nice restaurant, how could I put myself into their mindset, those murderers? I can't do it and I won't do it. I don't understand what's going on inside them, I can't see what's on the outside, even though it has often been on television and I only ever see what's going on there. The outermost [T/O for G.H.:—nope, won't land in English, you mean the *utmost*, dear EJ!] can be the innermost, but the innermost cannot be seen, I've mentioned it several times somewhere else, I think. You want people's deepest inside from me, but how should I know this? You want real people from me? Then you must turn to someone else! I am sure you have heard me say that many times before. You had to listen to all of it many times before. But it didn't hurt, did it? You are the last person I'd want to hurt!

Neither of the murderers likes to look to their borderlines and what they see might not even be their lines—and I don't mean mine—they cast themselves ahead and that didn't work, they didn't see where to kick ass, step on the gas and suddenly they had already gone overboard, no, no, not them, those were the others, I mean, they crossed the border, you mean, the line, they've reached their limits, whatever, earlier they hadn't even gotten to the border, their limits, my lines; OK, it was an experiment, a human experiment, as had been done a few times, many times, by Dr Mengele for example, who died peacefully in the ocean, in a beautiful, warm country, like many of his colleagues, who also spent their lives abroad and had a good time there. But this, after all and above all else is Germany, Germany everywhere, where many also lived happily ever after, well almost, until they were charged at age 94, which is hardly worth it. So there's one who charges them for what they had done in their lives, which they can hardly remember. No wonder no one gets killed in Germany, and if anyone does, then unintentionally, its name from now on shall be the whole world's, then no one will get killed anywhere, out of the opposite of fury, on the contrary, they were everything but furious, it's best we just drop it for now and pick it up again later, when you happen to look the other way. Well done, Germania! Germania! victims all gone and all perps too, from the mountains to the oceans, well done!, *Deutschland*, how now?, could it be you will trumpet ill-fortune? , no, you don't trumpet that, you simply trump it all, so it can make the normal or electronic news. Now I think I got lost. I must look something up again, flip through my brain, what I wanted to say, somewhere I said something about borders, lines, which are not to be moved, but looked across longingly to the other side, from the fatherland's side, which had wrapped their victims' clothing around its hips. That's the only way to get anywhere. Look up where your borderlines are, so we don't look the other way, you'd best be seen from behind. No turning around. Killing anyone shows a person his limits, good thing there are borderlines. Killing is so much work, not everyone can take it, let alone the victim. You can also be the loser in this, no question, and the question of *being* comes up and you get your come-uppance. You must report beyond the border, where the world puts its view up for grabs, to each his own—version, no, virgin, version of virgin?—a view he is looking forward to longingly: Now I forgot who whom or what, I probably meant the two murderers. The third one we'll forget for now, the other one did his job some other place, the two are not one single each, whose singularity lights up when he presses the remote or the flesh, they are à deux, but they are one as two, and that, for once, has nothing to do with a God. They don't see any borderlines, they have been moved, into the Nothing, into the Void, which they created themselves, into the vacuum, no, not a Hoover, he was his own brand of a sucker.

What sight do we have here? A gruesome one. We'd rather have a view, a nice one. No wonder one can't see any borderlines, not even if one's looking for a country with a soul, which, however, wants to look for someone else. Oh, well, they'll just be crossed, those lines, even if no one can see them, they get crossed now, otherwise we don't feel good in our skin. What kind of tragedy happened? Why did we stick our necks out so far? The world is out of joint, the earth a killing field. And lying on this field are already more than a hundred corpses. No one knows what *being* means. Can we ever know it at all? What we don't know is made knowable. If the shoe fits, wear it or get it to fit, there is some kind of spray for that. It was a pleasure, just a moment, I stepped over something here, was that the borderline?, just stepping to the side wouldn't have been enough for me, even though it would have been very easy. In a boundless world, one can get anywhere, in this one you have to first get gas where it's cheaper. It all depends. How do I name the stranger, who is everyone beyond the border, how can I call everyone by his name? There isn't enough room here. One could die thoughtlessly, not like these people who think about every detail of their death, calculating it, wishing for it and already looking forward to it. That guarantees extra points, a bonus; jail would only allow one visiting time, one attorney and, at the most, a jaw broken by the newest Aryan nation.

The earth screams: Don't touch me, or you'll end up like Antaeus, though in the short run he did not have to regret having touched the earth. I named him here, so now you can forget him. Our leading man here, Heracles, he got it, but it took a while. He could not defeat the former, because the fighter—one of many, but the strongest among those who were not yet in the slammer, thanks to his mother Erda, I mean Gaia—could regain his strength again and again by touching the earth, I am no hobby gardener, but I can understand this, I see earthworks everywhere, and so Heracles lifted him up and then his strength left him, bye bye birdie, power panties fell off Antaeus because he kicked so much in Heracles's arms, and all this in Libya of all places, he probably was even slippery from all that oil and because earlier he had also killed the father of the nation, that jolly good fellon, I don't know, but nothing good comes from there, nevertheless, the good fuel comes from there, but it wouldn't be able to drive the action here, I would constantly slip, because I wouldn't know in which hole I would have to put the oil, no worries, it will get even lower, at least with me! Here you find the depth you have been looking for, for so long. Oh no, it's no again, otherwise my knowledge will go the wrong way and the loss-of-memory disease—which, come to think of it, never caused much damage in others either, so why be afraid?—will once again take hold of me. OK, no more cheap jokes, they'll all be cut anyway, because they don't want to work! All my jokes have phone-in or phony jobs. But they never work in any case.

How do I name everyone or do I mean that one?, haven't I been stamped by every stay, no matter where, with Cain's mark on my forehead? I won't eat the food of the Gods, the young are picky, they don't swallow everything that's put in front of them, especially when they suddenly and unexpectedly believe in God. Then they nicely polish off their meal, otherwise they accept nothing from us anymore. And they don't think as is expected, except when they are told. And the old folks won't eat everything either, because they can't, no matter what they are told. There is a lot they simply can't digest anymore. OK, now I talked the way normal people do. Unfortunately, they are not doing it here. It isn't a God who wants to spare his sons their lives. Here the talk is of ropes, of fire, of defiance, of fury, wrath, of one who disdains arrows, no paths, I wish I could navigate this computer a bit better, but its paths are also unknown to me. The main thing is it knows them. I hope.

Wonderful. You left the mountains, why should I care? You say, you are well able to do horrible things if no one subdues you. You say you grow like lightning and strike where it really hurts. You say: no lightning, high fog or sun, I read that just now, and that this will be accurate most of the time, it won't have been the last time, it will repeat itself again and again, not only twice a day, you know, like the one about the broken clock. You think more frequently? You say, now you will kill wife and son. You say, you'll kill more people, but only those who deserve it. You ask about the pure voice of youth. It's just been here to give its vote—here the voting age starts already at age sixteen—but no one accepted it, because the booth was full.

No longer can we appear before father's and mother's eyes. That's what makes us so mad, so furious. No one shelters us anymore, spring will disappear, our youth will end the same way, sadly we won't notice when it happens. Good thing we won't live to see it, if we have to, still so young, put on the shroud of the dead. OK. At least we accomplished something before, we avoided the ossification of normalcy and it avoided us. Normalcy is defiant, because it wants to be the norm, while fewer and fewer people want to accept it. It wasn't our path, although they showed it to us. We always skipped the mediocre and always-the-same, and it always was a gas, gas in a jumpin' jackass, no shit!, no!, flash, in a flash we pounced on the weapons and BOOM!, BANG!, OUCH! Those Gods! No, not ours!—That one is the One all by himself—the others', those jokers, but whom do they draw? Ours, our God they know nothing about. That ban on images—that's also a lie. So there, now they know it, but you can no longer cash in on this knowledge. So do something with it now! Let's everyone draw someone he doesn't know. We'll stay calm then, but those guys will fly up like startled birds. But not under mother's dress will they want to find shelter, instead, they will raise their hand against us, because today we painted such a pretty picture, which she liked very much, but they don't like it at all. Did mommy lie and she didn't like it either? They will aim arrows at us, even though we feel safe, even though we throw ourselves on the floor and ask their forgiveness and change religion, even though we give them our women, no chance, they want us too, more than their own wives, we can't hide from them behind any locked door. There is always something one can do with women. Not with us. Oh, please, please, let us live! No chance! We would like to, but we can't, and no, we wouldn't like that either. It just isn't right. What should be not right with it? After all, we have proof, we have the video, if that's not proof how much we like to do it?! No idea. That was the Jews, not us. They forbid themselves so much so that they always know how what to do. They don't have much to do and still they make so much money. The Jews forbid

everything, Well, not us, we aren't Jews, they forbid themselves so much, so that they know the ropes. They can't even
write the name of God, since they can't draw anyway, that
would be something else, he would no longer be the Eternal
one. Whatever they would draw, it wouldn't be a God. It
might be an eye inside a triangle, a dove, what do I know
and besides, I slipped into the wrong religion without notic-
ing, no wonder, so then, let's just take this one, the new one,
well, it's not that new either, but it developed quite well,
though, unfortunately, it's stagnating a bit today. If you know
which one, you know more than I do; no worries, all reli-
gions develop fabulously these days; whenever one presses
ahead, the other follows immediately. Only we are somewhat behind and have to be set on fire, no, fired up. What
does the thinker say to this? The extraordinary must not
stand out, the utter—here, I must tinker with the thinker—
must be the Innermost. And those Jews shouldn't stick out
with their skullcaps or hats, we warned them.

Religion, in and of itself, is as useless as thinking. That's been
proven often enough, though not by the Jews. Not this time,
sorry. It was them, they did all that thinking which, I think,
is of little benefit to them, if all of them get killed. If they
don't give, they must be killed, we have no other choice. So
it goes. In their publicness—I mean, they still dare to show
themselves in public!—therein lies their audacity. It always
was them, be warned, it was them. They must say Adonai
when they name their God, while we must yell out the name
of ours before we kill, you notice: the *I* is already another
again, another division of religion, unfortunately, I don't
have the key to that one, but we do have this other key, we
want change, but then we don't like it. Yes, that happens very

quickly with us, kick in the door, done, crash through the door, done. I don't say: Can I crash at your place. But whoever is talking, says: We don't have to be ashamed, do we now, no one feels any shame anymore, so why us?, we yell out loud the holy name, we bellow, we see no reason to keep it a secret, I'd say, there also are a few steps between, which none of you chooses, you must think, everyone should know the name. You are right, and everyone does know as of late. It has become a household name.

We'll take those stupid flowers away, they can't lie there, only the dead are to lie here, especially one whom I won't have to mention here at all, as I am trying to group, so to speak, as many dead as possible, according to species, no idea which one, for one is already too many, but we must bundle, line them up, in the morgue or the pathology lab or whatever. It makes no difference in terms of the final result. There is a difference. They have certain restrictions, we have none. In God's name, which we may use, yes, must!, let's step aside, since our God is that huge. He really needs all the space he can get. He is even too big for us, but we understand what he means. Next to him there is no room for another one, especially not the one who killed his son. We say his name, he wouldn't kill anyone, he lets us do it. Thank you very much. We are young and can easily remember his name. That's what we say. We have been saying it all along. We say nothing else. We let ourselves be criticized by those—OK with me, go right ahead—by people far removed from the sort of suffering we want to bring. Damnation Damnation Damn Nation! And, yes, migration, that's also part of it, but it won't work out very often. Doesn't matter either, the ultimate sacrifice must be made at all times, we don't fight over reasons, not even with the trigger of the Kalashnikov, we just fight because we like it. Fighting is always good. Being and fighting is the same thing, that's why we don't mention it. We sacrifice our bodies and now we don't know what happened to them. We sprang from a man, yes, and from a woman too, but she doesn't exist anymore. Though, unfortunately, she has been necessary once. Mustn't offend a woman, otherwise, anything can be done with her. Father might have cut us off from lawlessness, he did right dying at the right time, because now we are right in everything we do. We are young and could do a lot more, if so desired, we have time. Such painfully sweet pleasure, our youth, a shimmering weir prepared for war to defend ourselves, for we must defend ourselves before anything happens, it's best we defend ourselves sooner, before anyone pushes us into misery, a frightfully coiled guard, a serpent, I think, and everything that happens to us happens not only to us. We like to share. Just imagine, our fantasies of omnipotence, our grandiosity, no, forget it, these words don't belong here, they knew it all along, that feeling of uniqueness and grandiosity, the young know everything, half-beings full of half-knowledge is what we are, the young, we only accept either/or and distinguish ourselves by hating any deeper reflection. We start running, we are told whereto and we instantly pass it on to our friends. We meet at XYZ and beat up people in the subway. Our 'half'-knowledge, would you believe Heidegger said it, he said this word—'Halbwissen' I swear, but I could also be wrong; I am writing this here, so you won't ascribe it to me!, half-knowledge, then, can easily be taken for faith, that's what we are dealing with, but don't get anything back for it other than death, which we manufacture ourselves, this production we do not outsource; we look at death—the burned, shot, cut to pieces—and we are quickly able to produce it ourselves, an apprenticeship is not a warship but it surely beats rubber rafts.

Yes, it is our faith which steers us around fatal pits and throws others in. That's been done countless times before, people still alive have been thrown into pits, beaten to death, shot—all good old, effective methods. We are coming, we are the up-and-coming and we are actually coming, why don't you understand that? Because we are not taken seriously, because we have no ground to stand on. But that's changing now. The access to that pit had been closed for a long time for those who wanted to get to the bottom of it and for those who had to. The run-off from this pit was clogged from all those bodies which had been there for a long time, now it is open, one can lift the cover, which, in fact, has already been done several times, we are the chute into this pit. How do I bring this People back to itself—it'll instantly become arbitrary and petty in its worldview, in everything coming out of itself , no, *all* by itself swimmingly. Why are you giving me this look? I am a different People, I am not a People at all, I am alone, I am not *we* either, can't say that about myself. Besides, someone else has written about it already.

Something drives us on. We are the many who reinforce each other, but going all the way we rather do alone. It's the only way to get to who we are and what we want to continue to be. We belong together, even though we go it alone with the weapon, all of us together we belong to our God who really is the greatest. We achieve unity—what belongs

together grows together—you cannot possibly misunder-
stand these historical forces, they have been explained to you
often enough by all kinds of people, from all sides, and
already in earlier times they could not be misunderstood,
except by the communists, but no worries, those won't come
back again, and they can't be restrained anymore either,
because they have moved into the unknown or become
Greeks. Ambition is man's strongest drive, that's a no-
brainer, I keep saying it, its strength might disappear in
you, but it disappears in the name of someone greater, the
greatest—just a greater cause would not be enough for us—
in the name of the greatest of all, which we utter, we do it
without hesitation, yes, let's do it!, anytime, especially when
we are planning to take someone out because no one can
see what's in it for us. Yes, that's the self-certainty of a People
once it loses the potential—no, that's another People—no,
which has lost possibilities to guard its very own, unique
determinateness, as the most questionable one and endure
it productively, that's a whole other piece of *Volk*, no wonder
the Germans lost the war, the way they dithered and
wavered! They could never do that with us. We are already
a piece of history, and sometimes we are two, three pieces
of history which, after the work's been done always get dispatched to eternity, airborne express. We've been uplifted
twice and that's how we feel, risen up high, we didn't need
a Heracles or Antaeus for a lift, twice risen because of sheer
ambition, zeal and craving for recognition, well, that's all we
needed: Here another one's rising up just now and over there
three get a lift across the border, where they've been drawn
to so intensely, even though everything sounded so foreign
to their ears at first, the women among them, I mean the

virgins, the other ones know it already, the virgins will soon find out how it is when nothing is foreign to one anymore. They'll find out from us warriors. Soon they will know. As soon as tomorrow. And they already know which house they will enter after their death. For death has been priced into their considerations, and afterwards it'll really be swell, no other than we will be the sacrifices we've made ourselves before and we won't even need a beautiful grave, we will be in another place, but we shall be, we'll get something better than a stupid grave. We will be scattered, not in the brain, scattered to the four winds, because we've been ripped apart, torn to shreds and now we can't get it all together again. We'll just sink, snorting and groaning and screaming, onto some dusty ground in front of some ruins we wrecked our-selves and then we'll rush to our God, whatever's left of us will hurry, maybe he'll pick us up in person. Who could have made it, this faith?, and twice at that, two strong faiths for two Brothers Grimmly, we always get new faith products delivered, that's why they get cheaper all the time no matter if we take them at face value or not and we also install them; we take out the old face and trash it and then we install your new faith free of charge, the new faith app, which you will never have problems with, it comes pre-installed, ready to go. That's a face that will last. If you want a new one, you'll just have to buy it and our God will then buy you, you'll see.

Those two. They will die too, this time not by the hand of the father, but indirectly, in a way. The father will be guilty, both could have easily lived longer, maybe not well, but they could have lived, by spending and wasting what's barely been saved. Anyway, we lucked out this time. Just a moment, let's take action and see what happens: No luck, after all. They took the car but didn't care to ask. It's all true—everything they've been told, after three weeks they all believe it as if they'd popped straight out of the Origin, and hadn't believed anything they'd been told before. Funny, they really believe everything, no, it's not funny. Now two brothers have no more worries, each has been given a piece of faith and now they want more of it, there is more where it came from, it's a miracle how fast it sticks in such a short time, but we work our conversions on the assembly line, and we don't get more, when it takes our creditors—who are meant to become unbelievable believers—three weeks to reach our God, while some can accomplish this in a few seconds, though only those who believed in him before and passed a training in how to leave one's house and soar?, sear?, no, disappear in thin air. But there are also the quick-minded, who catch on to it in two or three months. They get a bonus. Some become flyers, others high flyers. What was called a fight against sin has become a flight to win. But I would not want to bet on a winner. The dead don't have to be paid their winnings. Winners lose all. It didn't pay. But we don't get more out of it either, this is why we are speeding up the conversions. If we could do it in a week, we could still convert a few more, we do have time, but it must be done fast, the war needs soldiers. The kingdom of shadows needs inhabitants, the bike generator needs dupes to pedal it, so the light can be turned on there and the virgins brought in, who wouldn't be seen in the dark. The best would be missed. And considering how quickly they break, those soldiers of God, we can hardly keep up with converting.

We produce the front and we also produce the never flag-ging flow of progeny, we are their funding—, no, their founding fathers, we still have to procure the funds. Not a problem. They used to be the aliens in *Being*, now they are just alienating everyone. Just take a look at them! All the same and yet they are not. Their trousers shy away from the ground, and did you see that hand waving to us from its hiding? We couldn't even see the eyes belonging to it, too bad, they looked like something!, two kilos make up on them, that'll do. It was just a slit, can't throw anything in it. That's rich, the essence that comes with all of that, the essence of power, no, the essence of beings that requested the power and reserved it for themselves, it's been taken out, cleared for removal and we take what we are entitled to, our God will help us, we kill anything that moves, even though our God would like more people for his adoration, unfortu-nately we cannot fulfil this wish—period.

As for me personally, oh God, that's not even me, where is my mirror, that can't be! Well, whoever believes in him shall never die, oh no, this isn't me at all, unfortunately, this isn't me. I as the others, I may say I, for I am better than the others, I, personally—but I are many—don't ever believe that the hand of our Lord would do something unlawful and neither can we. We couldn't do anything our Lord doesn't like, and we would do even less what we don't like. Thus we don't notice that we want the same thing and therefore depend on each other. He is nothing without us and we are nothing without him. Oh yes, tits for *Tat*. Tit for deed. We are not our God and God isn't us. You better know this if you want to complain, if you want to want more pain. Our faith doesn't

figure in. We don't have any, we just call it that, it works
much better that way, we call it that because it's the most
one can have without knowing anything, and if one knows
something, the knowledge unfortunately collapses behind
us right away again and we don't find the way back across
the rubble, even if the sounds of flutes were to beguile us,
so what's with our belief now? Believing in the unrecognizable, which might not be unrecognizable, but how should
one ascertain this, if no one ever saw him?, by being a proud
fan—you can also make it an air-circulator, hot or cold, no,
both, two proud fans of the one and only God, who doesn't
need to be two because he can do it all. Yes, he can.

Every one of us is singular, even if we come in the plural of
twos or threes, it doesn't matter, everyone is one of his kind,
and if there are two of a kind, like those two!, all the better,
what did I want to say, we reject that. What are we rejecting?
Then we might as well reject our seed, so that no one raises
his hand against it. We reject tears, none of our deeds ever
got us to weep, maybe others, but not us. We flee after the
deed, but that doesn't matter either, we'll get to a much
more beautiful place later. You've never seen anything like
it! Neither did we. What do the others believe in? Let's keep
our ears open! They believe in something that will at some
time lead us to want to fuck mommy and kill the father,
everyone knows that, on pain of death and castration or one
of the two, they must not do it. This is a laborious procedure, I think it is an administrative term, some retroactive
legal action, I have heard the word many times, since the
Nazis had thrown out my father, and he had to be quite
proactive afterwards to get his due for what happened back

then. Anyone else anywhere, who wants to be administrated? Slaves. Victims. Infidels. We rather take you, weapons! We prefer activating you, because we already know beforehand what comes after, that's a big advantage we have. We don't need people, we need weapons. And perhaps people, who let themselves be served by the latter and then serve themselves. Servants of their weapons to wage a horrid war. We are weapons, but this does not solve the supply problems.

We kill, that's all, we keep doing it and we feel good about it, it's very easy with the right equipment, we almost regret that the father forbade killing, the father's legacy gets a bit tedious sometimes, he could have forbidden us something more difficult, that would have really been a sacrifice.

Now serpents are coming and don't know where to, they were dispatched so that we'd die and go down. But we don't do that. Our God demands that we take a few more with us when we die. The serpents can help, but that's all they can do. God thinks it's practical, then all goes at once, the dead with other dead in one piece of luggage, in tandem, in a double pack, a multi-pack. Well, we eliminated this pack!

No one may address us anymore in our pain, which we cause others but do not feel ourselves; no more talking to us by anyone. We have one single God, and now he unfolds in us, he has room there, we have his name on our lips, where did it go now?, what the heck have we got in our mouth?, spit it out at once!, we called him expressly by his name and he is coming, the love of the male child for his father makes him come, good, the precious name quickly spoken, very good, no lightning strikes, only a flashlight, it fought its way through the labors of the sun, it can hardly be seen and this love we must also forego unless we offer sacrifices to the father, whom else. Let all others be afraid, except our God who would never be in chains like yours and, rather than letting himself get beaten by others, he beats others. He is so great, one can't even say he is the greatest, for the greatest measures himself against something, and this one measures himself against no one, not in a fight, he doesn't need to, he is immeasurable, just look at the others, you can hardly see them next to him.

At all times all those Gods strive to have enemies and let them have it. But our Lord is the one and only master, I have never seen a second one. This is why I stress this so often. We go to great pains to die for him. And, big mouthed, we cause much greater pain. So many sons already born in vain and every day there are more. We trample around in earth's womb so that she would let us out. Then what? Well, we can do it, yes we can!, when you've been long enough up there on earth, you'll find the descent and we'll descend and kill our boss and ascend again, higher than before. You can see it yourself. It's already out, on the smartphone and on TV, us getting out. Even though we make ourselves small, so small that we can fit on your phone displays while we off others, my God, how often have I said this already! Whoever doesn't want to hear it, be silent or bug off, I beg your pardon, forgive this old bag and forget it. Only our God is great, he is the biggest, we don't even have to bring it up, he's got it up already and his wife is the best among women, blessed is she, guess who that is, you should know if you are one of us, not of me, I don't belong to any of that anymore.

We don't have to say more, because there is nothing more to say, at least for me. But we know that there is more to come. Now I am falling back into the original human shape and form, which I won't be able to leave anymore. I tried: nothing. I should have thought of this before. Besides, not one word here is true. That's how easy it is to deceive you! Even this palace split, its tower tumbled, no, I mean, I mean *from* the palace—those inside stumbled and split, no, what I really mean is: Under fire, the palace cracked and then it lost its tower and everything else. The refugees live in the basement, all that's left here are refugees and fighters. All others are dead or have left. I, however, am here and then there, wherever they threw me, but no one drew me, I draw myself, I am self-designed; I design myself and everything else; this robe is my design; so who's to blame now? You don't like it? You don't have to look at it, do you? That proves: There is no MORE than HE. There is only HE. There is no one more than is necessary through HIM. That proves nothing.

In his name we will carry out this operation on the cartoonists, an OP they won't survive. We are coming everywhere. I expressly do not say where to, because we are already everywhere, yes, me too, but I only watch it on TV anyway. We don't have to get there, we are there already, hold it, I cast my glance out the window for a change, no one returns it to me: It's true, we have arrived. HE, however, will always be and has always been. HE has always been here before us.

We are simply here, nothing else, but it wasn't so simple either. We shall die. Our *thrownness* will reveal terrible things to us, namely, that we could have done it too, but, once again, others have been authorized to do so. That'll do it for us. It was so horrific, we could have never done it had we not been we. But it could also have happened that we reached the end prematurely. This would have been effected by our God. And what did yours do? What has yours done during the time we were dying dutifully? Nothing either. He did nothing. That's one of those, who never get into the news, that God, he'd gone fishing or hung around some other place. Sounding out his opponents, but then he does nothing, just for the heck of it. He doesn't even know who his opponents are. We are his opponents, but do you think he would act on it? He has become big business, but doesn't do the dirty work himself. He is not a worker, he isn't doing anything. He does nothing, he just wants to play. Ours does something at least, no, I hear, he wants us to carry it out, take out our fury like a vicious animal, for which there is no leash and, inseparable as we are from him and the animal in us, we gladly support him in this. Among our brood, no one will pay, the house is painted in blood, the lord and master cheers, that one there too, all lords cheer, I would too, if I were a lord, and who pays for the father's hatred, which can't be extinguished? Well, I guess, someone will do it. Rigid but strong, this God sits on his eternal truth, on his eternal wisdom, on his eternal sofa set, which would have room for more than one, as the murders increase by the hour, the idea being that all the city's citizens will be drawn into the raging frenzy, and then, but then for real!, we turn on the proper device to look at ourselves, even though we have known ourselves for a long time, isn't it cool, we are on TV! But there's no one coming anymore. No one dares to. He sits there motionlessly, the lord, our master. We wouldn't invite servants anyway. He doesn't have to move, we do it for him. And his deputies are still here, too. Shoot! We won't have to tell you twice, do we now? They dispatched themselves here, but they used his protected brand name without paying for the rights, so now they've got to protect him themselves. The name doesn't tell us anything. He should use a different one. It doesn't have to tell anything. It has all been told.

In his name though, everything has been said, it's got it all, music or—if one wants to hear it—beautiful talk, yes, here it comes, directly to our ears, which we shouldn't sit on when it comes out. Technology advanced. We stay here. The in-between is an arcane march of electrons coming out of the player, but it works, the global player functions, you don't have to see them, you just have to hear them, those loony tones. Whatever. They line up nice and orderly and then there's nothing but these tones coming out of them because they can't do anything else; no tone may push to the front, that's how it is in life, always nicely one after the other. It comes on straight and pure, the tone, and God can do that too and much more, he doesn't get in one ear and out the other, he stays in, he stays, and he doesn't need any doors or windows, he doesn't need this new window either which can be installed so quickly, you don't know what hit you. Do you know this commercial? You don't have to, I'll tell you. You've hardly turned around for just a moment to do something, and suddenly—in place of the wall that's been there before in front of the heads facing it, and then only the empty hole that's been knocked into the wall—I put special emphasis on emptiness, as you can see—so then, suddenly, a window has been installed there, you don't know how, window glass plus frame and we bang against it pretty good because we didn't expect a window, which got built in so quickly, within seconds, not in the place where God lives, we were used to an empty hole there. In a flash, a window was there and in a flash it was already covered, if quite transparent. The person who banged against it didn't know that the glass had already been put in the hole. Ouch. Now there is something in there, which you can't see. Maybe my brain? I can't even describe a stupid commercial.

Now we know—we can tell from our raccoon eyes—that what they fitted in had to be glass, we, however, nearly threw a fit. This window also needs eye glasses, it seems, now that the sun shines through, finally. God is great and M. is his prophet, you must not draw him either, no, no, no! But it's not written anywhere that it is forbidden. I will find out the brand name of the window, so that I can tell you tomorrow in whose name something was filled in here. A pretty transparent procedure.

We support his election campaign, so where's the champagne, uhm, which campaign?, though it's really not a campaign, is it Le Pen?, Marine? she's a pain in the—, what marine?, they already deployed the marine?, no, that's not us, that's *the* U Ass A-OK, I'll stop it right there, in any event, we have no choice anyway. It's very easy, because, as mentioned briefly, no, pretty dragged out, I'm sure, no one really has a choice. When we are coming, no one has a choice. For us to

mock, to sport with, doomed to extinction are they. We take
care of it. We blast them out of their well-dreamed fortune,
which it isn't. Their father's speech gave hope to them once
too, no idea whom we mean, we only know that they were
drawing what they were not allowed to draw. Thus they
begat, no, made, that was the other one who was not made
but got to be, you gotta be kidding, where's that post. It's
not a post, that's why it doesn't have to topple over. Just as
the Nothing once dwelt in that window cave and then no
more, because something was put in there which could not
be seen. So, and now, those—whoever, it may be who had
lived here before—have nothing to hope for—now we are
here. Soon, just you wait, no one will be here anymore, no
one but us and our Lord, who simply is the greatest, and
that's what we are going for. He might be the greatest, but
allowing us to be featured in the 'Song of Murder'—a hit
today, tomorrow an even bigger one until at some point no
one can stand hearing it anymore—letting us be in it, in this
topical song, that's what we want. We want to become
known and we don't care who knows us. The main thing is
many. Everybody. Our Lord has to be in car-rich cities, in
garbage-filled subways, on level streets lined by stores, just
everywhere and he shall be everything, we wave the flag and
hand out death to anyone we catch. They won't enjoy their
fortune anymore, because we'll be even more fortunate,
we'll have won them all, the fights, we will have crushed
them, the enemies, already now no one can take our fame
away from us anymore and we shall own this country, all of
it, as we had prayed for to our father, maybe even inherited
it. We didn't even have to do that, for he always knows what
we want, and he always wants what we also want.

Your God has no idea of all this! Whatever you want, you are not to demand, you have to beg for it, pitiful you, and you do it only in the hope of eternal bliss, while we already switched sides here, to all sides, in order to fight, until we landed on the bright side in Paradise. Where we were before no longer counts, before we were nothing and nothing interested us, but now!, now we can demand something and exactly that which he wants to give us and has already given us.

The difference will be that we got it and you never did, you've always been just the questioners, we have the answers. We belong to the line of those who don't crumble and crave for anything new, for naturally we have all that already, we have everything you have, only more of it. It is old, but good. Good as new. At home we have the best devices, but this doesn't need mentioning here, we are those in the abyss who no longer look for the ground. Yes, we are more solidly grounded than all of those with strong convictions. You had your time, now it is ours and our missiles, remote-controlled hit even from afar, that is, from some distance, it can't be too great, and also at close range, we just hit everyone, we prayed for that to our father, and we've been getting it, for our father looks out for us, he is the greatest, no, the great One, since there is no one greater, we've already explained this and we have risen, without our courage and self-elation we wouldn't get up to Him, his mighty throne, it's not that easy to get there, how else do you think we came to do our bloody deeds? They are not coming to us!

On the run, your lives are rushing ahead, yes, there they whizz by! You won't catch up with them anymore. The Kingdom of the Dead has opened, the ladder is here, the barque is here, the boat; yesterday a few hundreds more drowned, but this won't happen to us. We've made our dogpile. They shake their empty body bags and then they shake their weapons, no idea where they got them, I won't describe them, not more than has been necessary so far, I am not Homer, not by a long shot could I go into such detail, let alone come anywhere near him, and the Holy One will never bless our covenant because I bolted already. Life, yes, well, you didn't get it from us, of course I don't mean Homer and myself, but we are also fighters, we chase death's cart that races ahead, no idea what's driving it, maybe that new drive no one had known before. We would have never entrusted it to you, the fighting, the killing, and it must be squeezed into one second so that the soul still has time to catch the bus, it's a very tight connection, what's in the schedule is often wrong, if the trolley is late by just one minute, the bus is gone. The soul has to walk, it's quite a distance. So it flies, it has fled already, fled from its owner when he stopped paying attention for a moment. We should have given you something less perishable than your life, so you could hold on to your God even then, yes, hop on that board with the wheels and off you go, so you get the chance to leave the country at least once. But he will shake you off like the tree its leaves and you will spin into the Nothing.

You don't know it yet, but all of you must die, that's a given. Listen to me, I won't say it a third time. What, it's already the tenth? Well, I don't care. If it were up to us, all of you must die, but all the others, who are dead already—you can ask them, they have the same opinion. And so it happened that on the seventh day it got light, but no one was there, he spoke somewhere, exactly, and on that day, which I made sure to mark in the calendar, he said something like that: And God rested on the seventh day from all his work. Why does he specially mention this? Those who finally get to rest also rest from all their work, as God does from his. No one rests, only God is allowed to. The soul, which we received from him flies around merrily, it acquired a taste for flying, that drone, that parasite that does nothing but suck us dry and pursue its hobbies, but for the soul it's quite a different story. It flies a few more salti and soli, the soul, before it has to report to the boss. OK. And now nobody can talk to us anymore, because we are busy, today is not Sunday or whatever the infidels call it, what is and shall be and what we don't believe, because our God says something else on another day, another time. High up in heaven, bravely conscious and proud of our guilt, forgive us, please, only our God is allowed to be conscious of his guilt and declare: I don't have any. It does not behoove us. We have no consciousness except for whatever he has given us and, to cut a long story short: We know that we must kill the cartoonists, yes, the Jews too, but everyone knows that one must kill the Jews, not only we, everyone knows it here in the hall and on their devices at home as they used to say, now everything is a device and everywhere, no distinction gets made between our smartphones and us, but between our God and us it does.

Meanwhile you can still consecrate earth's short dream to the air, it won't do you any good. From daybreak till night you will still be free of sorrow, by morning it will be too late. Pray now, before doom is upon you. OK, pray, let's go! Then you'll be free no more, for our freedom starts right then! Then no one will consider your wishes anymore, only ours, time won't accept any wishes either, where would it be, if it had to constantly avoid those wishes, which it would even know by then?, for time is void of wishes, and soon we'll be voided as well. Please deposit all wishes in this social forum, yes in that one too, oh, but there is one already, hold it!, that one just sends what he has been doing and filming with his ActCam, a video stick would have been more practical, easier to handle, you will notice it and you will also be able to see it on the screen, big and small, I mean the screens, that no one's fulfilling those, the wishes, big and small, file them right here, please, no one reads them there, but here millions are reading them, who also believe in us yet can't bring themselves to rob their parents, to soil garments with blood, hack off a hand that's ready to serve, stone a woman without hesitation, yes, a man too, one won't make a difference, both at the same time would be best, it takes fewer stones; we take advantage of it, what?, well, that we can do all that. We even must do it. We take advantage of everything, we use the fora, we use the net to its limits, which it doesn't have, no one draws the line, except if we were in China or Persia or Russia, wherever, but we are not there, where we would have to circumvent borders, here our nice net welcomes us all, we love it. That's so much better than the love for a father who has to deny us everything, so that we want still more, instead of talking to the father we talk

to strangers, that's such fun! One doesn't have to be consid-
erate. Our wishes are flying away, and after a while—wanna
bet?,—the fate we bring others will abduct us up into the air
and smash us to the ground again. It will make sense for us
after we come back to our senses. But we don't care for that
woman. She is crazy!, but that's not my fault, I am her, after
all, that woman. Even *we* couldn't care less about *us*, rather
it's all in God's hands. It's in his hands only.

Fortune's abundance, great fame, whom did they ever
remain true to? But on one single day they all stayed with
us, they were hacked into the ground, riddled with bullets,
knocked over and thrown down, we did it on solid grounds,
and now we are famous for it, in every world, not just in this
one, verily, I say unto you, you can have this too, if you work
hard at it. I say: Farewell, you idiots! However, one thing is
clear, you won't have seen us for the last time, yes, yes, keep
screaming, I don't care and you'll see and it will be the last
thing you have seen. But new ones are coming, again and
again, like us, popping up out of nowhere, like dream visions
in sunlight, you better watch out for those! They are even
more furious than us, every one more furious than the other.
Beware, a wall is revealed here, a wall of people, who are
one. This is why I am calling them: Wall. If only one drops
out of it, people will die. Your father is supposed to have told
you that? I can't see that. Forbidding as well as punishing
were exclusively his domain, the man who snuck in front of
the camera next to mother and child. This wall crumbles,
the father must have noticed that he doesn't fit into this picture, but the father's not the issue here. He could be anyone
who is shown to us. He can even live in half a bra for a piece

of wafer or a black garbage bag for a beard one has to kiss. Always with those beams around it so one knows what it is. No, it's not garbage. But that wouldn't stop it.

The room darkens and then it dissolves and then it can't be seen anymore. We are losing ground, we can't see anything, could also be hell, which might not be bad, we are freezing. Whatever, you can really get furious now, because you can no longer see your borders and draw the line, now you can pile it all up on our arms, the wardrobe of your fury, because it's only external, isn't it. No idea where I should put it. It's completely dark, but a red glow is coming from somewhere, no idea if something is burning again, something is always burning somewhere around here, humans too, the fire takes everything, it's the least picky of us all. Fury jerks and twists like a mean beast, it's alive all right, let me tell you, it never keeps still, I felt it through and through. People are literally prying it out of my hands, even though they came in with completely different jackets, they want to leave with that one. And if you'd always,—too late as always—pay respect and attention to them, the furious, who keep loading their arms with suits, dresses and ruffles no, rifles and other firearms around the clock, what Glocks?, those rock!, no, cut that bull!—, balls?,—shit!, I don't have balls; so let's just have one., a concert, maybe, a party? Look around, you'll be able to crash some event, some other place, start moving, shit happens everywhere—it won't do you any good anymore. The fans have already been hit. The innocent blood has already been shed, come back tomorrow, there'll be more where they came from. And the deity stands right behind you, don't turn around or it may be your turn, because you crossed the death path of the God and he was just about to pass. Who does this woman belong to? You don't know? That was murder, not a fight. Women and children don't fight! No shit! The adornments of death mean nothing, this orange overall means nothing, this death-dress here, which no one has taken yet—it means nothing, no matter what color it is, no friend will protect them, they will all be dead. Dead dead dead.

An antistrophe, wasn't there one already, oh well, then this one is also anti:

Nothing on earth coming from a God is safe, no question about that. There you believe you can storm a city, kill a People, you can kill also all others including those who aren't even part of it, and then we blew it. We blew the killing, because we did not want to tolerate a God. We didn't need him, but realized too late that we could have possibly used him. Maybe we can get a used one? Here, the others have the home-turf advantage, for their home is God and they always carry him with them. But if we had one, we too would start killing right away. Oh, if only we had him already! But ours hangs naked and exposed on that cross, while he could also hang with us. Nevertheless, whenever we get another one assigned to us, one just a bit more aggressive, we start killing right away, sometimes after just three weeks of training and exams in believing. Basically anyone can do it, let no one address us in some weird way or it'll be his turn. The extraordinary must not attract attention, that's why you never see us coming, this quilted coat is a good protection, the outer-xx-most must be the innermost

and this is how we normally do it, normal folks do it differently, they are doing it their way. They don't see us, they
don't see us coming, we could be anyone. This kind of
feather coat, stuffed with natural animal products, everyone
wears it nowadays, you can lift that from any wardrobe, yes,
also the cap and the scarf, everyone wears them, well, we
also are like everyone else, we are not recognized, we have
nothing to recognize us by, this way we keep our bravery to
ourselves until the very end. So then, when no sees us coming, we can always pull it off, we always succeed destroying
what was born in pain. Mom and the born, they always were
two. Dad skedaddled. No, not on skis, he used a rope, our
heavenly father would have managed without one. So much
pain and then more pain. Everything living must die. Sure
thing. Our lot is dying. We know we must die, you and I,
those we fight against must die, though we must too, but—
we will have it better afterwards, the others won't. We want
what we must anyway—take flight, oh children, hurry away!
But it won't do you any good. So these people—blessed are
the peacemakers—, they can already pick up their certificate
of inheritance and they can watch something on Late Night
TV, unless they die already in the morning, then they can
call on their God and his prophet a hundred times, though
we don't even know, does he have any of those prophets?,
does he know anything about them?, it's generally said he
does, OK, but those prophets were weak, the proof is that
now one God has become inferior to the other. For them,
he was just a forerunner of the Lord, even though that one
stood only in shallow water, showing off. For us, he is just
the third-to-last of the prophets. He can't effect anything and
this forerunner has long been replaced by the runner who

committed suicide in public and still got to the Father in heaven who allowed such a thing. That's crazy. We can't possibly become a part of this! They've got to go! All of them! All Peoples who trust their God to protect them, off with them. We are secular, even though we've got our God, the never-touched Origin and beginning, we don't need him anymore, though we scream out his name, but we don't need him at all, because the never-touched Origin and beginning—where a phantom creature creates havoc all around in its unrecognizability will also end some day—we won't be there. No problem. We also believe in something, we take it often and with pleasure, we don't have anything else, even if we don't know what it is, but we take anything and only look afterwards what it was. And most of all we like to believe in the dark, after all, we don't know ourselves either. So, the Origin lies behind us, not that long ago, but, in any case, it won't return, we are here and we are young, aren't we!, but it's behind us once and for all, the beginning, we are just waiting for the end, hold it, it's coming, it's coming!, and that's good. But not yet. We too must die, but not now. Now others are dying. Then us. Everything at its time. And this time is ours anyway.

So there they sought shelter under those, how shall I put it?, wings, like chickens, God one big chicken, I am sorry, I don't want to ridicule him, that would really be the last thing I'd want to say, which would be welcomed by many, but ridiculing him—others are already doing it and getting punished for it, with more death. No, not chickens; birds, the kind that take us under their wings or lend us their feathers for such a coat, though they'll never get them back again, birds do that—I don't want to insult anyone here—nestling against a God's faithful chest, and he kicks them out of the nest again, where they have already dragged some furniture, is this a tub, a toilet, a kitchen? No. So I say: Not consumed by flames are we, that's the least of evils, our enemies' mockery, that's the biggest evil, a greater evil even than death. Yes, mockery is evil, greater than us in any case, it must be atoned for with strongest measures. Our names, however, will be carried into the world afterwards and put down some place, until other names will get to be known. It will have been worth it, no? Only our God will know where we lay, which row, which lot and this will do for us. He knows where he should pick us up. Mockery is the greatest evil, that's why we don't like it, mockery destroys us, therefore those mockers are the first ones we kill. This is how we did it in the war, we killed so many, but it would be unbearable to us had we to die a cowardly death. We kill before the mocking gets started. Only a few times they got ahead of us. Better before, but we don't always nail it. We can't always execute before something gets said. We can't be everywhere at the same time. Not cowardice is holding us back, neither is lust for life. Mockery must go. The first one to go. As is the mocker. His neck offers itself to the MG, there's shooting, murdering, hurling down from the third floor, hurrying up to the first floor, we ask for the address and then we bring death for pictures, so that more pictures will be made with passions anchored in them and we can kill even more.

Now the situation—well, finally!: What is man? What is man compared to his picture! It makes no fucking difference, we can look at a man, and yes, a woman too, anywhere and

everywhere, even in the image,—yes, always taken with pleasure, even when the apparatus is stuck on a stick, an impaled
hand camera, it's looking good already, just wait when you
see the image, much better than before we had a stick, that
is, if the camera won't break down before. We won't lose
anything by posting it online later, on the contrary, we'll
duplicate ourselves. If we are lucky, millions of times! The
image stays! It stays everywhere we put it, it can never be
misplaced, it stays in the device and leaves at the same time
and it can show up anywhere, every time you click on it. This
is where it will stay, yes, please, any time. And it will stay as
long as you like, the image is actually eternal, because the
net loses nothing. If it gets deleted somewhere, it can still
be seen in other places, the image, in thousands of places.
One can always see everything. What? A door creaked. It
cannot do that. Nothing should alert the Invisible to us, he's
got other things to do.

I hear water. We cannot tolerate any of this. We can't tolerate it, because on principle we are no tolerators, we are ter-
minators. We are not stupid. We are not tolerant on
principle. What? Are you kidding? You are coming from a
God? I told you, it creates the greatest insecurity if you don't
say which one, so don't do that please or provide informa-
tion about yourself and your only child, which he allegedly
killed. Come from some other place, it doesn't matter which
one, no, it does matter, we must know, because we won't
tolerate it, unless it is our God, then welcome, brother, sis-
ter! Are you saying you've never heard of this, what for do
you need notebooks to write this down? What for do we
need teachers? We do need them, but only if you want to be

a leader and not teach anyone anything, that would be too laborious. Ye that labor and are heavy laden? Well, those must belong to someone else, another tourist group, follow the red umbrella, we follow the raised purse, the stick, the colorful scarf. Poor woman, her arm's hurting already. Did we already mention something about dragon seed? Already forgotten, although it's been just two minutes ago. No, it was at the beginning, and that was hours ago.

You said it, I am sorry, but you did say it, you did so against the levelling and the limitless application of the leader principle, you said it, no one understood it, because a leader is needed in the unknown, and this will be carried out: The sons of the earth—whom the God of war, emptying the dragon's jaws with kicks and punches, well, he simply broke out his teeth, right?, so he could scatter the dragon seed and so he did, he sowed them, like we said—and those unspeakable ones, who do not want to talk to us, sowed the dragon seed, no, not sawed, with the jigsaw a heart into the outhouse door, they don't make those anymore, they don't even have outhouses, a bucket will do, a bucket's enough if they limit the intake of food a bit, they'll have to, they do, then one bucket will do for the whole night, the runs of the Jews, who have already been on the run from us a long time and for all times and that won't change anymore, those runs can also run down the wall and drip into the lower beds, that's why it's better to have the bed on top, oh no, now the dragon's top tooth fell down on top of it all. But he's got more. That wasn't his only tooth. No God shall ever rule us with impunity again, and no country and no People and no continent and no boss and no earth and no land and no sea.

We are off the leash, no, we don't get off the leash, I believe, this is a river, I think, no idea where it is, but we've been let off the leash. That'll work. Yes, I believe it works.

Please protect us from vicious attacks!

Hear, dear God, my voice in my lament, if you can stand it, it really doesn't sound very good, not good enough for you. We are too small for you, guide me, oh God. Protect my life, please, from those horrific enemies, there are so many, I have no overview. Hide me from the attacks of evil, from the raging of the rivers and the evildoers, who sharpen their tongues like swords, but then make the swords even sharper. They like it hot. Oh yes. They aim their poisonous tongues at us like arrows, but when they stop saying anything, when they only say the name of their God, which they are so crazy about, then they get even crazier. They've nailed their mad attacks, they hit their targets quite often, too often, I have to admit, unfortunately, they are talking about how they want to lay out cords and set snares, and they talk and they talk— well, let's put it that way—they say the following: First they always say the name of their God, that's simply part of it, even though it can't be so simple to remember the name, when one's thoughts are already elsewhere, how many will they get this time?, why aren't they afraid?, if not of us, then at least of their God? Why do they have no fear?, how can that be?, who can see them? You surely can see then! You see everything! Please tell us where they are, are they already climbing up the stairs, could they crack the door code or did someone show it to them? Makes no difference. They've got evil in mind and keep it still secret, only afterwards billions

can see it in the networks, in the dragnets you cast over
them, so that they'd believe someone is listening to them,
which, unfortunately, is not the case, on the pillion of the
net or what do I know, I think riding two up is prohibited
these days except for killings. Where else? Wherever else
they watch evil. They also mail their evil to editorial offices,
where they then kill the editors—why mail anything that
won't get to a recipient or millions of those, it's all the same,
no, it's only a few thousand, there are more than that, but
one time only! Total insanity! Who can see them, we said it
already, so we ask again, who? They have evil in mind, we
already said that too, God, you don't want to always listen
to the same thing, you'd switch the channels, but there's a
commercial on this one at the moment, and there are shopping shows on another, you, on the other hand, open the
garbage can instead, before we are finished praying, and we
must throw in all the junk, because only you are important,
no one else. You don't have to lift a finger for it, it all ends
up in one sewer or another. So there you hit them with an
arrow, at least you hope you got them, and suddenly they
are thrown to the floor. Their own tongue brought them
down before the arrow, and the time it took them to film it
all, no, it took no time at all, the expensive adventure cam
runs automatically, that's what we'd also need. But why
would their own tongue bring them down so that anyone
watching would mock them? OK, first we were doing the
mocking and then they tripped over our tongues, and then
it was us, we tripped over our own tongues, God, how could
you let it happen? But we will be here longer, even if we are
not around anymore. You will watch out for us, God, even
when we won't be here, and all humans will be afraid, they

are afraid now and they'll say: God did it! And we swear that's not true. Don't believe it when you hear it. He didn't do it, even though you believe you can recognize the work as his, it wasn't. The righteous will rejoice in the Lord and bank on him, the building will collapse nonetheless, the joy will remain, but in heaven, with the one, the only righteous one who is there, because God was so pleased with him that he took him along, and whatever pleases him he wants to look at again and again. He doesn't seem to be so pleased with us. Maybe because we want to take revenge? Instead of being righteous, though revenge would be in order in such cases, I just don't know where. On the wall? No, something else hangs there. And all pious hearts will pride themselves on him, I forgot in whose names they will boast this time, they did not give his name, how then should we know what happened? Well, I don't care. The Godless are supposed to go to hell, all heroes, who are forgetting God are to get the hell out of here as well. No idea. The hope of the deceased should not be lost, but, unfortunately, I can't find it, what can you do. Rise, oh Lord, so humans won't get the upper hand. It happened already, unfortunately. Now they rule over you, Lord, but you still must have a servant, whoever, or you wouldn't be a master. And you haven't yet noticed, no idea, what! Well now. Let all the heathens, no, heroes, no, heathens, so everyone except us, be sentenced before you. Why don't you do it? Lord, cast a terror on them, so that they realize that the heathens, no, clearly the heroes, it doesn't really say the way it's written here, but it must refer to the heroes, and Lord, cast your terror on them, so that they realize that those are something too. Here it says humans. That they are human, it says so here. Exactly, that's exactly what they say here. But there is no one here.

I ask myself, if it's not the other way around, if I did not jump the gun, if it hadn't been you right from the beginning. I don't answer myself. Terrible are you, not telling me, a terrible judge, yes, when you set out to judge. Well now, get started, that thou helpest all on earth, really everyone, who suffers in some way, who also suffer like everyone else, then no one will be left yet again. Everything was ready to go, everyone went to his death, no one around anymore. But you like it the way it is, you like it that way. When people rage, does it get you anything? What? Exactly. It gets you honor and if they rage even more, you are prepared as well, Lord. You want them to bring you gifts—to you, the terrible? Well, OK, so they bring them. It won't pacify you. It will make you more furious. It will be the wrong gifts. Only a few shreds of flesh, not worth freezing them. You will throw them in their faces, and then you will throw out their faces with the pies that somehow landed on them. And the heads right after. This kind of thing happens very quickly once you are in full swing. They are burning down all houses of God for you, and, when none are left, they'll also burn down all the other houses. You hurl them to the ground, but they go on, on this slippery ground you had put them before, so they would slip and fall, as you presaged. But the ground stops no one, unless he lies under it. As a matter of fact, that's what I thought already, there he lies, among many others, underneath many others, and the ground itself had been held open by someone's shaking arms, until all of them, really all, were in it. Everything will disappear, most of it is gone already. One can see the knives rising as if humans were the thickets of the forest. One can see them set a shrine on fire, defiling it to the ground, the home that is registered in your sacred name can no longer be leased, Lord. As a landlord, you are a dead loss. The water damage alone cannot be repaired; I won't even mention the loss by fire. You didn't imagine it this way, did you? The dragon in the sea, not even purebred, a chunk of a beast, who was poured out too by mistake, the Leviathan, a colleague of death, with whom you love to play, you put your hand between his jaws to check whether he's still got all the fillings and bridges, which you paid for, yes, you are playing with death and the monster, it's all a game for you. You play with evil and let it even win from time to time. As to the other vermin, there's nothing left of your fondness. Thrown to wild animals? Who?, Whom?, I forgot, stop it with all your accusations! Be honest now, as long as there will be an arm to be raised: Who is supposed to be able to live here? Not even if he gets paid for it! The door has been kicked in, no one could step in now and anyway, the door has never been in the way. Not really. The water wrecked everything. Rubble everywhere. God, to extinguish the fire burning in us you let springs and streams burst forth and now no one can bear it here, that's a fact, there isn't even a cooking facility or water or a toilet. You didn't think of that before. Building this house was an investment that did not pay, now everything is ruined, even before anyone had moved in. Good job indeed! For that you let strong rivers run dry or burst out, according to your will and threw whatever people to wild animals. Everything belongs to you, but so what? Now what? What are you left with? Maybe it was worth it after all, because everyone paid? They paid in advance, those poor idiots. They paid too soon. A nice change from the usual, as people pay too late most of the time, but at least they know for what. Day and night, which you also made, yes, both, what will happen to them? You won't get them wrecked that fast. Yes, and the sun and the stars, everything yours. And, most important of all: You drew the line. But no one seems to see it. They go here, they go there. They go around it. You made summer and winter, only no one can feel it. It is all the same. When everything is dead, it's all the same.

Euripides, *The Madness of Heracles*

Andreas Marneros, *Irrsal! Wirrsal! Wahnsinn. Psychose und psychische Konflikte in Tragödien*

Hans-Joachim Behrendt, *Justitia prohibitora. Das väterliche Gesetz und die oedipale Szene*

Florian Freistetter, 'Wir wissen wo Du wohnst' (Article quoted from the Austrian magazine *Profil*)

Sigmund Freud, *Zur Gewinnung des Feuers*

Of course Heidegger, too. A few scraps from *The Black Notebooks, 1931–1938*.

King David's *Psalms*

Klaus Theleweit, *Das Lachen der Täter*.

Thanks to Maria A. Stassinopoulou